FUN KNITS
for kids

Also by George
Hostler
Wit Knits

FUN KNITS
for kids

OVER 40 DAZZLING DESIGNS | **FOR CLEVER CLOTHES – FROM BABYHOOD TO TEENAGE**

GEORGE HOSTLER

**J. M. Dent & Sons
Limited**
London   Melbourne

This book is set in Plantin Medium by Input Typesetting Ltd
Printed in Spain by Graficromo S.A., Cordoba for
J. M. Dent & Sons Ltd
Aldine House, 33 Welbeck Street,
London W1M 8LX

British Library Cataloguing in Publication Data

Hostler, George
  Fun Knits for Kids
  1. Children's clothing   2. Knitting – Patterns
  I. Title
  646.4'07   TT820

ISBN 0–460–04715–9

CONTENTS

Acknowledgements

The author and publishers would like to thank the following people for their help in the production of this book.

Knitters

Mary Cartledge
Pauline Hill
Anne Hostler
Elsie Ivenson
Mrs Seely
Jean Stalker
Pat Thompson

Pattern Writer

Chris Lancashire

Illustrations

Sara Sliwinska

Pattern Grids

Clive Sutherland

Photography

Francis Loney, assisted by Steve Nichols

Make-up

Kevin Christian

Hair

Nigel Barnes

Models

Catherine Allkins
Charles Allkins
Stefano Barolo
Aphra Brandreth
Benet Brandreth
Saethryd Brandreth
Andrew Cartledge
Anthony Dorment
Angus Gore-Andrews
Emma Hills
Rowley Hudson
Kia
Daniel Matthews
Glen Power
Scott Power
Alex Shellard
Toby Shellard
Lizzie Woolfenden
Tom Woolfenden

USEFUL INFORMATION

Machine Knitting

The patterns accompanying each garment in this book have been written for hand knitting. However, the majority of them, expecially the picture knits, are quite suitable for machine knitters who have the type of machine which allows for hand selection of needles or has an intarsia carriage.

Instructions for the picture or pattern-making techniques vary from one machine to another and will normally be covered in the manual under Fair Isle or intarsia knitting headings.

Experienced knitters will notice that many of the garments illustrated have been made up on machines. The yarn tensions used are exactly the same as those of the hand-knitting instructions, so the written patterns can be used with complete confidence.

Don't forget that in machine knitting the back of the knitting faces you as you are working so any design you are following will be reversed. This probably doesn't matter unless you are using letters or words, in which case you must work the design backwards. This is not as difficult as it sounds and you will soon pick up the technique.

Measurements

Carefully check the measurements given for each garment and adjust them if necessary.

Tension

Each pattern gives the tension to which the original garment was knitted as a number of stitches and rows to a 4 in. (10 cm) square. Check that your tension is correct by knitting a square on needles of the recommended size. If your tension is incorrect the garment will not turn out the right size. If you have fewer stitches than the given tension, use needles a size smaller than those recommended in the pattern; if you have more stitches than required, use needles a size larger.

Casting On

Make a slip loop at one end of the yarn and slip it on the left-hand needle. Insert the right-hand needle into it as shown in the diagram, wind the yarn round the right-hand needle, draw a loop through with the right-hand needle and transfer it to the left-hand needle. This forms one stitch. If it is very loose, pull the yarn to tighten it.

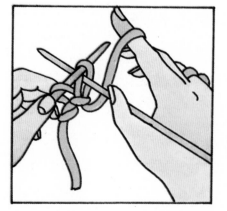

Continue until you have the required number of stitches, working into the last stitch on the left-hand needle each time.

Casting Off

Knit the first two stitches of the row. With the point of the left-hand needle bring the stitch on the right of the right-hand needle over that on the left and slip it off the needle. Knit one more stitch and repeat the procedure. Continue until only one stitch remains. Cut the yarn and pass it through this stitch to fasten off.

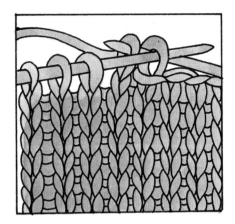

Stocking Stitch

Most of the garments in this book are knitted in stocking stitch, which is created by alternate rows of knitting and purling.

Knitting

Hold the needle with the cast-on stitches in your left hand and the empty needle in your right hand. With the yarn at the back, insert the right-hand needle into the first stitch on the left-hand needle from the front of the stitch to the back (i.e. away from you). Bring the yarn under and over the point of the right-hand needle, draw a loop through, and slide the first stitch off the left-hand needle, keeping the new stitch on the right-hand needle. Continue to the end of the row.

To knit the next row, transfer the right-hand needle to the left hand and start again.

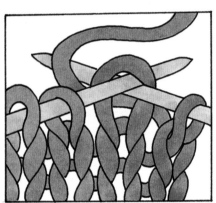
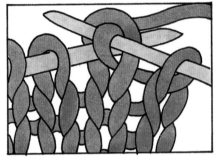

Purling

Hold the needle with the cast-on stitches in your left hand and the empty needle in your right hand. With the yarn at the front, insert the right-hand needle into the first stitch on the left-hand needle from the back of the stitch to the front (i.e. towards you). Take the yarn over and around the point of the right-hand needle, draw a loop through and slide the stitch off the left-hand needle, keeping the new stitch on the right-hand needle. Continue to the end of the row.

To purl the next row, transfer the right-hand needle to the left hand and start again.

Joining in Yarn

If possible try to join in a new ball of yarn at the beginning of a row. Any long ends which are left will be useful for sewing up.

Sewing Up

Invisible Seam

An invisible seam is used for the side and sleeve seams of a garment where the seam runs in the direction of the knitting.

Place the two pieces to be joined edge to edge, matching them row for row. Secure the yarn at one end, pick up a stitch on the same side of the garment, then take the needle across to the other side and insert it under the thread that connects the first and second stitches of the row. Draw the needle and yarn through and then insert them through the same thread on the opposite piece of knitting. Draw the edges of the two pieces together firmly but not too tightly. Continue until the seam is finished, then fasten off the yarn.

Backstitch Seam

A backstitch seam is used where the seam runs across the direction of the knitting, such as in the shoulder seams or along shaped edges.

Place the two pieces to be joined right sides together, lining up the edges and rows. Secure the yarn at one end and then sew from right to left, moving one stitch to the right (or backwards) on the side facing you and two stitches to the left (or forwards) on the side away from you. Continue until the seam is finished, then fasten off the yarn.

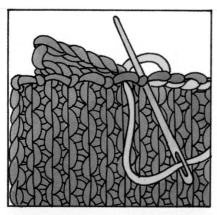

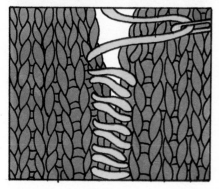

Pressing

Before you start, check any special instructions given with the yarn. Each piece of the garment should first be pinned out to the correct size given in the pattern, wrong side uppermost. Put a damp cloth over it and, using a warm iron, press down on the wool, then lift the iron. *Do not move the iron over the cloth, as in ordinary ironing.* Repeat until the whole piece has been pressed, then press the remaining pieces.

Abbreviations

MC. – main colour, con. – contrast, cm. – centimetre, in.(s) – inch(es), K. – knit, P. – purl, st. st. – stocking stitch (1 row knit, 1 row purl), patt. – pattern, inc. – increase, st(s). – stitch(es), cont. – continued, beg. – beginning, RS. – right side, WS. – wrong side, foll. – following, rem. – remaining, alt. – alternate, dec. – decrease, incl. – including, tog. – together, rep. – repeat, rev. – reverse, sl. – slip, psso. – pass slip stitch over, tbl. – through back of loop, g.st. – garter stitch, yfwd. – yarn forward, col. – colour.

Needle Conversion Chart

Continental – mm	UK	USA
2	14	00
2¼	13	0
2¾	12	1
3	11	2
3¼	10	3
3¾	9	4
4	8	5
4½	7	6
5	6	7
5½	5	8
6	4	9
6½	3	10
7	2	10½
7½	1	11
8	0	12
8½	00	13
9	000	15

American terminology

Most knitting terms are identical in English and American usage. The exceptions to this are listed below, with the English term used in the book given first, followed by the American term. Stocking stitch (st. st.) = stockinette stitch; yarn round needle (y.r.n.) = yarn over needle (y.o.n.); cast off = bind off.

Yarns and Suppliers

Suppliers of the yarns used in this book are listed below.

Patons & Baldwins
Alloa
Clackmannanshire
Scotland FK10 1EG

Metallic Yarns
Silverknit
Park Road
Calverton
Nottingham NG14 6LL

4-ply supplied mainly by
R. J. Cole Ltd
'King Cole Anti-tickle Finish'
Superwash 4-ply
This yarn can be obtained by mail order from the following:

West Yorkshire Textiles
PO Box 175
Bradford
West Yorkshire BD10 0UD
Tel. 0532 502519

Metropolitan Sewing Machines
Stone Lane
Wimborne
Dorset
Tel. 0202 881611

Knit Well Wools Ltd
116 Sunbridge Road
Bradford
West Yorkshire
Tel. 0274 722290

Overseas readers:

Most of the patterns in this book use 4-ply yarn. Any other 4-ply or double knitting wool can be used instead as long as you check for tension before knitting the garment.

Patons & Baldwins:

Coats Patons (Australia) Ltd
PO Box 110
Ferntree Gully Road
Mount Waverley
Victoria
Australia

Coats Patons (New Zealand) Ltd
Mohuia Crescent
PO Box 50/140
Elsdon
Porirua
Wellington
New Zealand

Susan Bates Inc
212 Middlesex Avenue
Chester
Connecticut 06412
USA

Patons & Baldwins Canada Inc
1001 Roselawn Avenue
Toronto
Ontario
Canada M6B 1B8

Patons & Baldwins South Africa
(Pty) Ltd
PO Box 33
Randfontein
1760 Transvaal
South Africa

Pingouin

Pingouin Wools
29 Old Bailey
London EC4
Tel. 01–248 1002 (retail and mail order)

French Wools Ltd
7–11 Lexington Street
London W1 (for information about
main stockists)

Promafil Corp
9179 Red Branch Road
Columbia
Maryland
21045
USA

C. Sullivan Ltd
3 Ralph Street
Alexandria
Sydney
NSW 2015
PO Box 249
Australia

S. I. L. A. F.
Via Corregio 19
20149 Milano
Italia

Yarn conversion chart:

	Australia	New Zealand	Canada	USA
Patons 4-ply	Bluebell/ Patonyl	Bluebell/ Patonyl	Beehive 4-ply Fingering/ Jaeger Alpaca	

LITTLE SWEETHEART

A complete outfit for the youngest member of the family – with the heart worn anywhere but on the sleeve.

ANGEL TOP

MATERIALS

Yarn (for all sizes) 2 × 50g 4 ply main colour (white) 1 × 50g contrast A (fuchsia)
8 small buttons
Needles 1 pair 2¼mm (UK 13) 1 pair 2¾mm (UK 12)

MEASUREMENTS

To fit Birth (3: 6) months
Chest 16 (17: 18) in, 41 (43: 46) cm.
Length 9¼ (9¾: 10¼) in, 23 (25: 26) cm.
Sleeve seam 2½ (3¼: 3½) in, 6 (8: 9) cm.

TENSION

30 sts and 40 rows to 10 cm square on 2¾mm needles (or size needed to obtain given tension).

BACK AND FRONT

(Worked in one piece).
With 2¼mm needles and MC cast on 147 (153: 165) sts.
Work ½ in (1.5 cm) in garter st. (every row K).
Change to 2¾mm needles and starting with a K row, work in st. st.,
Next row – (Buttonhole row) K to last 5 sts. K2tog. yfwd K3.
Next row – K5, P to last 5 sts, K5.
Keeping 5 sts at each side in g. st, work 2 (6: 8) rows.
Commence patt. as follows:
Next row – K52 (55: 61) sts., K 1st row of patt. from chart 1, K to end of row.
Next row – K5, P47 (50: 56) sts, P 2nd row of patt. from chart 1, P to last 5 sts, K5.
Cont. working rows of patt. from chart as placed. At the same time working 6 more buttonholes as before 11 (12: 13) rows apart. When work measures 5¾ (6: 6¼) in, 13 (15: 16) cm. from beg. ending with a p. row, divide for armholes.

○ To divide for armholes
With RS work facing, sl. 39 (40: 43) sts each side onto a spare needle.

Cont. on 69 (73: 79) sts in centre for Front.
Keeping patt. as set cont. straight until work measures 7½ (8: 8½) in, 19 (20: 22) cm from beg. ending with a P row.

○ To shape neck
With RS work facing K30 (32: 35) sts, turn, leave rem. sts. on a spare needle.
*Cast off at neck edge on next and foll. alt. rows 3 sts once, 2 sts 1 (1: 2) times and 1 st. 4 times. [21 (23: 24) sts].
Cont. straight until work measures 9¼ (9¾: 10¼) in, 23 (25: 26) cm. from beg. ending with a P row. Cast off.
With RS work facing sl. next 9 sts onto a holder. Rejoin yarn to next st. and K to end of row. Work 1 row. Complete to match first side from * to end.
　Rejoin yarn at back edge to 39 (40: 43) sts for Left Back. Keeping 5 sts in g. st. cont. straight until work measures 8¾ (9¼: 9¾) in, 22 (23: 25) cm. from beg. ending with a P row at centre back edge.

○ To shape neck
Cast off 9 (9: 10) sts. at beg. of next row and 9 (8: 9) sts. at beg. of foll. alt. row. Work 1 row.
Cast off rem. 21 (23: 24) sts.
Rejoin yarn at armhole edge to 39 (40: 43) sts. for Right Back and complete to match Left Back reversing neck shaping and keeping 5 sts. at back edge in g. st.

SLEEVES

With 2¼mm needles and MC cast on 46 (50:54) sts. Work ½ in (1.5 cm) in g. st.
Change to 2¾mm needles and starting with a K row, work in st. st.
Inc. 1 st at both ends on the 2nd, then every foll. 4th row to 62 (62: 68) sts.
Work straight until sleeve measures 2½ (3¼: 3½) in, 6 (8: 9) cm from beg.
Cast off.

NECKBAND

Join shoulder seams.
With RS work facing, 2¼mm needles and MC, pick up and K20 (20: 21) sts along Right Back neck, 16 (16: 17) sts, down Right Front neck, 9 sts from centre front, 16 (16: 17) sts up Left Front neck and 20 (20: 21) sts along

Left Back neck [81 (81: 85) sts]. Knit 5 rows.
Next row – (Last Buttonhole row) K to last 5 sts, K2tog, yfwd K3.
Knit 4 rows. Cast off.

TO MAKE UP

Press work according to yarn instructions.
Join sleeve seams. Sew in sleeves. Sew on buttons.

HEART PANTS

MATERIALS

Yarn (for all sizes) 2 × 50g 4 ply main colour (white).
Small amount contrast A (fuchsia).
Needles 1 pair 2¼mm (UK 13) 1 pair 2¾mm (UK 12)

MEASUREMENTS

To fit Birth (3: 6) months.
Hips 20 (20½: 22) in, 51 (52: 56) cm. (finished measurements)
Length (waist to bottom of leg) 6¾ (7¾: 8¾) in, 17 (20: 22) cm.

TENSION

30 sts and 40 rows to 10 cm square on 2¾mm needles (or size needed to obtain given tension).

FRONT

Left Leg.
With 2¼mm needles and MC cast on 42 (44: 46) sts.
Work ½ in (1.5 cm) in g. st.
Change to 2¾mm needles and starting with a K row, work in st. st.
Cont. straight until work measures 2(2½: 2¾) in, 5 (6:7) cm from beg. ending with a P row.

○ To shape leg
Cast off 2 sts. at beg. of next row and 1 st. at beg. of foll. alt. row. (ending with a right side row).
Leave rem. 39 (41: 43) sts on a spare needle.

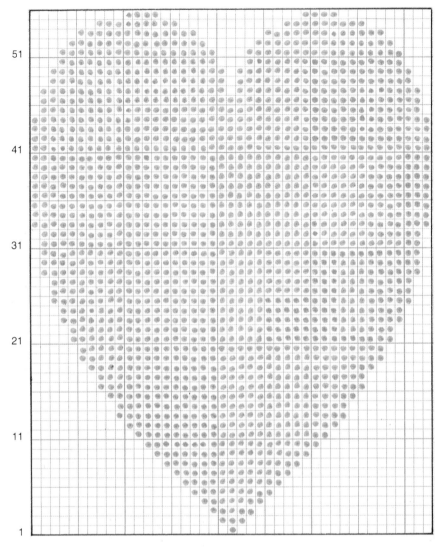

PATTERN 1

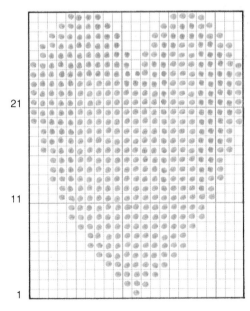

PATTERN 2

PATTERN 3

Right Leg.
Work as for Left Leg reversing shaping and ending with a right side row.
Next row – With WS facing place both sets of sts. onto a 2¾mm needle (shaped edges to centre), P 38 (40: 42) sts., P2tog, P 38 (40: 42) sts. [77 (81: 85) sts].
Cont. straight until work measures 6¾ (7¾: 8¾) in, 17 (20: 22) cm ending with a K row.
**Change to 2¼mm needles and work 5 rows in g. st.
Next row – (Waistband eyelet row) K1 (3:1) sts,* K2tog, yfwd K6, rep. from * to last 4 (6: 4) sts, K2tog, yfwd K2 (4: 2).
Work 4 more rows g. st. Cast off.

BACK

Right Leg
With 2¼mm needles and MC cast on 46 (48: 50) sts. Work ½in (1.5 cm) in g. st.
Change to 2¾mm needles and starting with a K row, work in st. st. Cont. straight until work measures 2 (2½: 2¾) in, 5 (6: 7) cm from beg. ending with a K row.

○ **To shape leg**
Cast off 3 sts. at beg. of next row and 2 sts. at beg. of foll. alt. row. Work 1 row. Dec. 1 st. at beg. of next and foll. alt. row. Leave rem. 39 (41: 43) sts on a spare needle.

Left Leg
Work as for Right Leg reversing shaping and ending with a right side row.
Next row – With WS facing place both sets of sts onto a 2¾mm needle (shaped edges to centre), P38 (40: 42) sts., P2tog, P38 (40: 42) sts. [77 (81: 85) sts].
Work 2 (4: 6) rows.
Commence patt. as follows:
Next row – K42 (45: 48) sts, K 1st row of patt. from chart 2, K to end of row.
Next row – P12 (13: 14) sts, P, 2nd row of patt. from chart 2, P to end of row.
Cont. working rows of patt. from chart 2 as placed.
When patt. completed, cont. straight until work measures 6¾ (7¾: 8¾) in, 17 (20: 22) cms. from beg. ending with a P row.

○ **To shape waist**
1st row – K to last 5 (5: 6) sts, turn.
2nd row – P to last 5 (5: 6) sts, turn.
Rep. last 2 rows 3 times more, leaving 5 (5: 6) sts unworked at end of each row.
With RS work facing rejoin yarn to first set of sts at beg. of shaping and K across all sts.

11

Complete as for Front from ** to end.

○ To make up

Press work according to yarn instructions.

Join gusset, side and leg seams.

Twist 3 strands yarn together to make a tie and thread through eyelet holes in waistband.

HEART CARDIGAN

MATERIALS

Yarn (for all sizes)
2 × 50g 4 ply main colour (white)
1 × 50g contrast A (fuchsia)
4 small buttons
Needles 1 pair 2¾mm (UK 12)

MEASUREMENTS

To fit Birth (3: 6) months
Chest 16 (17: 18) in, 41 (43: 46) cm
Length 9 (9½: 10) in, 23 (24: 25) cm
Sleeve seam 4½ (6: 6¾) in, 11 (15: 17) cm

TENSION

30 sts and 40 rows to 10 cm square on 2¾mm needles (or size needed to obtain given tension).

BACK and FRONTS

(Worked in one piece.)
With 2¾mm needles and MC cast on 155 (161: 174) sts.
Work ½ in. (1.5 cm) in g. st.
Next row – (Buttonhole row) K3, yfwd K2tog, K to end of row.
Next row – K5, P to last 5 sts, K5.
Cont. straight and in st. st., keeping 5 sts at each side in g. st and working 2 more buttonholes as before 21 (23: 24) rows apart. When work measures 1¼ (1½: 2) in, 3 (4: 5) cm from beg. ending with a P row, commence patt. as follows.
Next row – K56 (59: 65) sts, K 1st row of patt. from Chart 1, K to end of row.
Next row – K5, P51 (54: 61) sts, P 2nd row of patt. from chart 1, P to last 5 sts K5.
Cont. working rows of patt. from chart 1 as placed, keeping 5 sts at each side in g. st and working buttonholes where necessary.
When 14th (16th: 18th) row of patt. 1 has been worked commence patt 2 on Left Front as follows:
Next row – With RS work facing K56 (59: 65) sts, K 15th (17th: 19th) row of patt 1 from chart, K24 (26: 33) sts, K 1st row of patt 2 from chart, K9 (10: 11) sts.
Next row – K5 sts, P4 (5: 6) sts, P 2nd

12

row of patt 2 from chart, P24 (26: 33) sts, P 16th(18th: 20th) row of patt. 1 from chart, P to last 5 sts. K5.
Cont. working rows of patt. 1 and 2 from charts as placed. At the same time when work measures 4½ (5: 5½) in, 11 (13: 14) cm from beg. ending with a P row, divide for armholes.

○ To divide for armholes
With RS work facing sl. 40 (42: 45) sts at each side onto spare needles.
Cont. on 75 (77: 84) sts in centre for back.
Cont. straight until work measures 8½ (9: 9¾) in, 22 (23: 25) cm from beg. ending with a P row.

○ To shape neck
Next row – K32 (33: 36) sts, turn, leave rem. sts on a spare needle. *Work 2 rows.
Cast off 11 (11: 12) sts at beg. of next row. Work 1 row.
Cast off rem 21 (22: 24) sts for shoulder. With RS facing sl. next 11 (11: 12) sts onto a holder.
Rejoin yarn to next st. and complete to match other side from * to end.
Rejoin yarn at front edge to 40 (42: 45) sts for Right Front. Cont. straight, working buttonhole as before, until work measures 6¾ (7¼: 7¾) in., 17 (18: 20) cm from beg. ending at front edge.

○ To shape neck
Cast off 8 sts at beg. of next row. K to end. Work 1 row.
Cast off at neck edge on next and foll. alt. rows 3 sts once, 2 sts 3 times and 1 st 2 (3: 4) times [21 (22: 24) sts]. Work straight until length measures same as back to shoulder ending with a P row.
Cast off rem. 21 (22: 24) sts for shoulder.
Rejoin yarn at armhole edge to 40 (42: 45) sts for Left Front. Working rows of patt. 2 as placed complete to match Right Front reversing neck shaping.

SLEEVES

With 2¾mm needles and MC cast on 42 (46: 50) sts.
Work ½ in (1.5 cm) in g. st. Starting with a K row, work in st. st. At the same time inc. 1 st at both ends on every 3rd (4th: 4th) row to 64 (68: 74) sts. Cont. straight until work measures 4½ (6: 6¾) in, 11 (15: 17) cm. from beg. Cast off.

NECKBAND

Join shoulder seams.
With RS work facing, 2¾mm needles and MC pick up and K28 (29: 30) sts from right front neck, 33 (33: 37) sts from back neck and 28 (29: 30) sts from

left front neck. [89 (91: 97) sts].
Work 3 rows g st.
Next row – K3, yfwd, K2tog, K to end.
Work 2 rows g. st. Cast off.

TO MAKE UP

Press work according to yarn instructions. Join sleeve seams. Sew in sleeves. Sew on buttons.

HEART SHOES

MATERIALS

Yarn small amount 4 ply main colour (white)
Small amount contrast A (fuchsia)
2 small buttons
Needles 1 pair 2¾mm (UK 12)

MEASUREMENTS

One size only.

RIGHT SHOE

Top of shoe
With 2¾mm needles and MC cast on 13 sts. Starting with a K row, work in st. st. Work 4 rows.
Next row – K3, K 1st row of patt. 3 from chart, K3.
Next row – P2, P 2nd row of patt. 3 from chart P3.
Cont. working rows of patt. from chart as placed. When patt. completed work 4 rows MC. Break yarn and leave sts. on a spare needle.

Main Part
With 2¾mm needles and MC cast on 40 sts. Work 3 rows g. st.
4th row (Make buttonhole) K37, yfwd K2tog, K1.
Work 4 more row g. st.
9th row – Cast off 17 sts, K to end [23 sts].
Next row – K23, K14 sts down left side of top, K13 sts from spare needle and K14 sts up right side of top [64 sts].
Work 10 rows g. st.
Next row – Cast off 15 sts. K to end.
Next row – Cast off 37 sts. K to end.
Cont. in g. st. on rem. 12 sts and work 3½ in (9 cm).
Cast off.

Work Left Shoe to match, reversing shapings.

TO MAKE UP

Do not press.
Join seams. Sew on buttons.

HONEY CHIL'

Sensational stripes make the wearer of this outfit look like the bee's knees.

MATERIALS

Yarn – Sweater 2 (2: 2: 3) × 50g 4 ply main colour (yellow)
1 × 50g Contrast A (black)
Pants (for all sizes)
1 × 50g 4 ply main colour (yellow)
1 × 50g Contrast A (black)
Elastic for waist
Needles 1 pair 2¾mm (UK 12)
1 pair 3¼mm (UK 10)

MEASUREMENTS

To fit chest 18 (19: 20: 22) in. 46 (48: 51: 56) cm.
Sweater
Length 10¼ (10¼: 11¼: 12) in. 26 (26: 28: 31) cm
Sleeve Seam 7 (8: 9: 9¾) in. 18 (20: 23: 25) cm
Pants
Hips 20 (20½: 21: 24) in. 51 (52: 53: 61) cm. (finished measurement)
Length (waist to bottom of leg) 10¾ (11¾: 12: 12½) in. 27 (30: 31: 32) cm.

TENSION

28 sts and 36 rows to 10 cm square on 3¼mm needles (or size needed to obtain given tension).

STRIPE PATTERN

2 rows con. A, 2 rows MC.

SWEATER

BACK

With 2¾mm needles and MC cast on 68 (72: 76: 86) sts.
Work ¾ in (2 cm) in K2 P2 rib.
Change to 3¼mm needles and starting with a K row, work in st. st.
Work the 4 rows of the *stripe patt* 4 (4: 6: 7) times, then work 2 rows con A. ★
Rejoin MC and work 58 rows.
At the same time when work measures 6¼ (6¼: 6¾: 7¼) in, 16 (16: 17: 18.5) cm from beg. place col. marker at each end of last row (to mark position for armholes).
★★ When MC rows completed, rejoin con A and work 2 rows con A, 2 rows

MC, 2 rows con A. Break off con A.
Change to 2¾mm needles and with MC work ½in (1 cm) in K2 P2 rib. Cast off in rib.

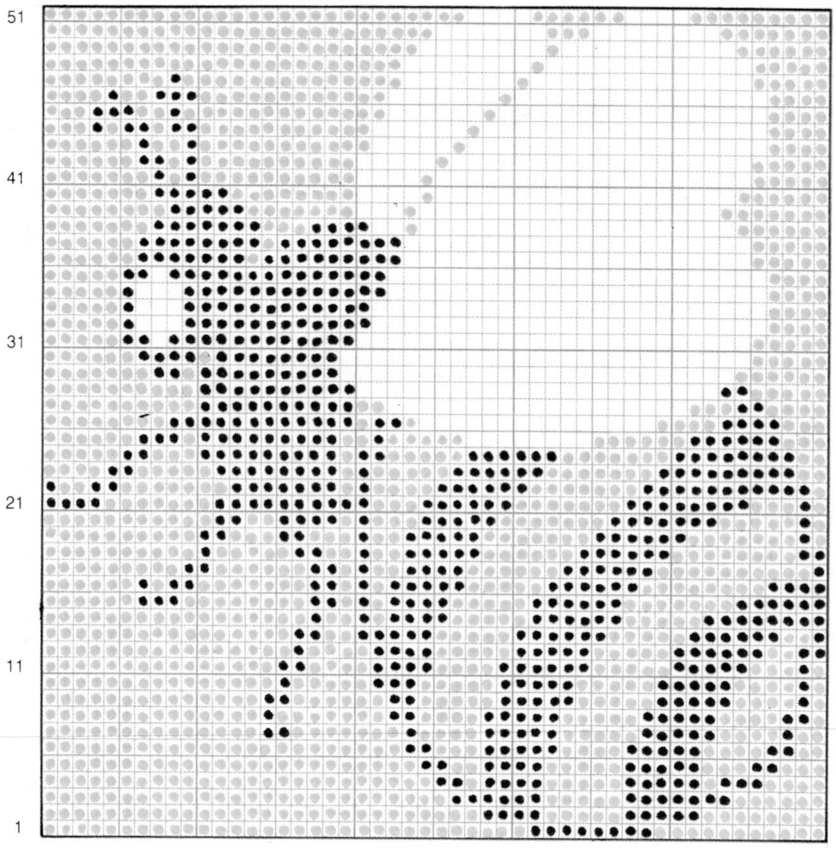

FRONT

Work as given for back to ★. Rejoin MC and work 4 rows.
Next row – K9 (11: 13: 18) sts., K 1st row of patt. from chart, K to end of row.
Next row – P9 (11: 13: 18) sts, P 2nd row of patt. from chart, P to end of row.
Cont. working rows of patt. from chart as placed. At the same time when work measures 6¼ (6¼: 6¾: 7¼) in, 16 (16: 17: 18.5 cm) from beg. place col. marker at each end of last row.
When rows of patt. completed work 3 rows MC.
Complete as for back from ★★ to end.

SLEEVES

With 2¾mm needles and MC cast on 42 (42: 46: 46) sts.
Work ¾ in (2 cm) in K2 P2 rib. On the last row inc. 12 (12: 12: 14) sts evenly. [54 (54: 58: 60) sts.]
Change to 3¼mm needles and starting with a K row, work *stripe patt.* (throughout) in st. st.
At the same time inc. 1 st. at both ends of every 0 (18th: 16th: 10th) row 0 (3: 4: 7) times [54 (60: 66: 74) sts].
Cont. straight in *stripe patt.* until work measures 7 (8: 9: 9¾) in, 18 (20: 23: 25) cm from beg. Cast off.

TO MAKE UP

Press work according to yarn instructions, omitting ribbing.
Join shoulder seams 1¼ (1½: 1½: 2¼) in, 3.5 (4: 4: 6) cm at each side. Sew sleeve top between col. markers. Join side and sleeve seams.

PANTS

BACK

With 2¾mm needles and MC cast on 68 (72: 76: 84) sts.
Work 1¼ in (3 cm) in K2 P2 rib ending with a WS row.
Change to 3¼mm needles and working *stripe patt.* (throughout) in st. st., commence waist shaping as follows.
1st row – Sl. 22 (24: 25: 28) sts onto Right needle, with con A K24 (24: 26: 28) sts, turn.
2nd row – With con A, P24 (24: 26: 28) sts, turn.
3rd row – Sl. 4 (4: 4: 5) sts from Right needle onto Left needle, with MC K 32 (32: 34: 38) sts turn,
4th row – With MC, P32 (32: 34: 38) sts turn,
Cont. in *stripe patt.* taking 4 (4: 4: 5) sts. at each side into patt. every 2 rows 4 times more, then taking 2 (4: 5: 3) sts. at each side into patt. 1 time.

Cont. in *stripe patt.* on all sts until work measures 7¼ (8: 8¼: 8¼) in, 18 (20: 21: 21) cm, measured at side edge ending with a P row.

○ To divide for legs

Next row – K30 (32: 34: 38) sts. Cast off 8 sts. K30 (32: 34: 38) sts.
Work each leg separately.
*** Cont. in *stripe patt.* until leg measures 2 (2¼: 2¼: 2¾) in, 5 (6: 6: 7) cm from cast-off row, ending with 2 rows con A.
Change to 2¾mm needles and with MC, work 1½ in (4 cm) in K2 P2 rib. Cast off in rib.
Rejoin yarn to inside edge of leg and complete as for first leg from *** to end.

FRONT

With 2¾mm needles and MC cast on 68 (72: 76: 84) sts.
Work 1¼ in (3 cm) in K2 P2 rib. ending with a WS row.

Change to 3¼mm needles and starting with a K row, work *stripe patt.* (throughout) in st. st. commencing with 2 rows con A. Cont. straight until work measures 7¼ (8: 8¼: 8¼) in, 18 (20: 21: 21) cm, from beg. ending with a P row.

○ To divide for legs

Next row – K 30 (32: 34: 38) sts. Cast off 8 sts. K 30 (32: 34: 38) sts.
Complete as for Back from *** to end.

TO MAKE UP

Press work according to yarn instructions omitting ribbing.
Join side and leg seams. Fold waistband in half and sew down on wrong side. Thread elastic through waistband.

SWEET HEART

Children's comics inspired the designs for the next two sweaters. Will the wearer of this one match up to the words on his chest? The less brave should also make the one on page 18 so there's always a sweater to match the mood.

SWEET HEART

MATERIALS

Yarn 2 (3: 3) × 50g 4 ply main colour
Small amount { 4 ply Contrast 1
                4 ply Contrast 2
Needles 1 pair 2mm (UK 14)
1 pair 2¾mm (UK 12)

MEASUREMENTS

To fit Chest 19 (22: 25) ins, 48 (56: 64) cms
Length 10½ (12½: 14½) ins, 27 (32: 37) cms
Sleeve 7¾ (8¾: 10¼) ins, 19.5 (22: 26) cms

TENSION

30 sts and 40 rows to 10 cm square on 2¾mm needles (or size needed to obtain given tension).

STRIPE PATTERN 1

(in rib).
2 rows MC, 2 rows Con 1, 6 rows Con 2, 2 rows Con 1, 2 rows MC.

STRIPE PATTERN 2

(in rib – neck border)
2 rows MC, 2 rows Con 1, 2 rows Con 2, 2 rows Con 1, 2 rows MC.

BACK

With 2mm needles and MC cast on 72 (84: 96) sts. Work *Stripe patt.* 1 in K1 P1 rib. On the last row inc. 12 sts evenly [84 (96: 108) sts].
Change to 2¾mm needles and with MC work in st. st.
Cont. straight until work measures 6½ (7½: 8¾) in, 16 (19: 22) cms from beg. ending with a P row.

○ To shape armholes
★ Cast off 4 sts at beg. of next 2 rows.
Cast off 2 sts. at beg. of next 2 rows [72 (84: 96) sts].★
Cont. straight until work measures 10¼

(12½: 14) in, 26 (31: 36) cms. from beg. ending with a P row.

○ To shape neck and shoulders
With RS of work facing K30 (35: 41) sts, cast off 12 (14: 14) sts, K to end.
Work on last set of sts. as follows:
Next row – P
Next row – Cast off 14 sts at neck edge, K to end.
Next row – P.
Next row – Cast off rem. 16 (21: 27) sts. for shoulder.
Rejoin yarn to remaining sts. at neck edge and complete other side to match, reversing shaping.

FRONT

Work as given for Back until work measures 2¾ (4: 6) in, 7 (10: 15) cm from beg. ending with a P row.
Next row – K15 (21: 27) sts. K 1st row of patt. from chart, K to end.
Next row – P14 (20: 26) sts. P 2nd row of patt. from chart, P to end.
Cont. working rows of patt. from chart as placed. At the same time when work measures same as back to armholes, ending with a P row, shape armholes.

○ To shape armholes
Work as given for Back from ★ to ★, keeping patt. over sts. as set. Cont. straight until work measures 8¾ (10¼: 12½) in, 22 (26: 31) cm from beg.

○ To shape neck and shoulders
With RS of work facing K30 (35: 41) sts, cast off 12 (14: 14) sts. K to end.
Work on last set of sts as follows:
Work 1 row.
Cast off at neck edge on next and foll. alt. rows, 4 sts once, 3 sts twice, 2 sts once and 1 st. twice.
Cont. straight until work measures 10½ (12¾: 14½) in, 27 (32: 37) cms. from beg. ending with a P row.
Cast off rem. 16 (21: 27) sts. for shoulder.
Rejoin yarn at neck edge and complete other side to match reversing shaping.

SLEEVES

With 2mm needles and MC cast on 42 (48: 52) sts. Work *Stripe patt.* 1 in K1, P1 rib. On the last row inc. 12 sts evenly [54 (60: 64) sts].
Change to 2¾mm needles and with MC work in st. st. Inc. 1 st. at both ends

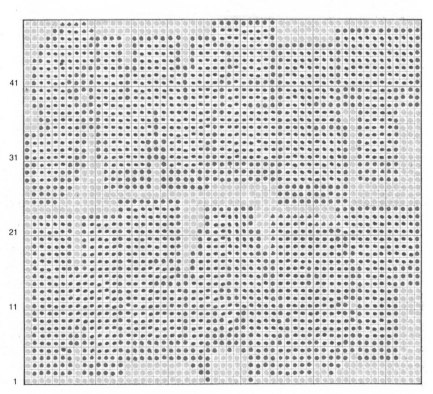

on the 6th and every foll. 10 (8: 7)th row until there are 66 (78: 90) sts. Work straight until sleeve measures 7½ (8¾: 10¼) in, 19.5 (22: 26) cm from beg. ending with a P row.

○ **To shape top**
Cast off 7 (8: 9) sts at beg. of next 8 rows.
Cast off rem. 10 (14: 18) sts.

NECKBAND

Join left shoulder seam.
With RS work facing, 2mm needles and MC, pick up and K 96 (106: 106) sts evenly around neck edge.
Purl one row.
Work *Stripe patt.* 2 in K1, P1 rib.
Cast off loosely in rib.

TO MAKE UP

Press work according to yarn instructions omitting ribbing.
Join right shoulder and neckband.
Join side and sleeve seams.
Sew sleeves into armholes.

LITTLE RASCAL

Just right for a tomboy

This pattern is identical to the previous one, with the exception of the motif on the front. Follow the Sweet Heart pattern, therefore, but set the pattern of the motif like this:

FRONT

Work as given for Back until work measures 2½ (3¾: 5) in, 6 (9: 13) cm from beg. ending with a P row.
Next row – K 14 (20: 26) sts. K 1st row of patt. from chart, K to end.
Next row – P14 (20: 26) sts, P 2nd row of patt. from chart, P to end.
Cont. working rows of patt. from chart as placed and complete as for Sweet Heart sweater.

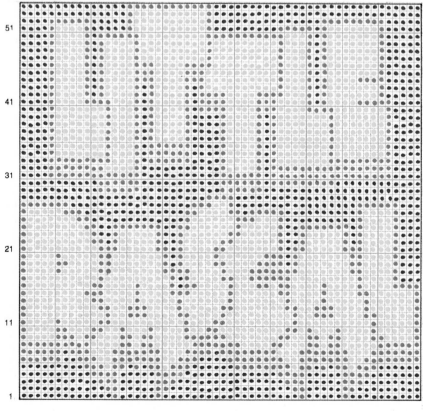

SLUGS AND SNAILS...

...and puppy dogs' tails – that's what little boys are popularly made of

MATERIALS

Yarn 4(5: 5: 6) × 50g 4 ply main colour (white)
1×50g contrast A (black)
Small amounts contrasts B-green, C-purple, D-red, E-orange, F-yellow, G-royal blue.
Needles 1 pair 2¾mm (UK 12) 1 pair 3¼mm (UK 10)

MEASUREMENTS

To fit chest 24 (26: 28: 30) in., 61(66: 71: 76) cm.
Length 16 (16½: 19½: 20½) in, 41 (42: 49: 52) cm
Sleeve seam 11½ (12½: 14: 15) in, 29 (32: 36: 38) cm.

TENSION

28 sts and 36 rows to 10 cm square on 3¼mm needles (or size needed to obtain given tension).

BACK

With 2¾mm needles and MC cast on 90 (98: 106: 114) sts. Work 2in (5 cm) in K2 P2 rib.
Change to 3¼mm needles and starting with a K row work stripe patt. in st. st as follows.
24, 26 in. size.
*Work 2 rows C, 20 rows MC, 2 rows D, **20 rows MC, 2 rows E***, 20 rows MC, 2 rows F, 20 rows MC, 2 rows B, 20 rows MC, 2 rows G, *Rejoin MC to complete work.
28, 30 in. size.
Work as for 24/26 in. size from * to *. Cont. stripe patt. as follows 20 rows MC, 2 rows C, 20 rows MC, 2 row D. Rejoin MC to complete work.
ALL SIZES
At the same time when work measures 10 (10½: 12½: 13½) in, 26 (27: 32: 34) cm. from beg, ending with a P row shape armholes.

◯ To shape armholes
Keeping stripe patt. correct, inc. 1 st. at both ends of next and every foll. 10th row, 5 (5: 6: 6) times.
[102 (110: 120: 128) sts.] Work 3 (3: 5: 5) rows straight.

◯ To shape shoulders
Cast off 5 (6: 6: 6) sts. at beg. of next

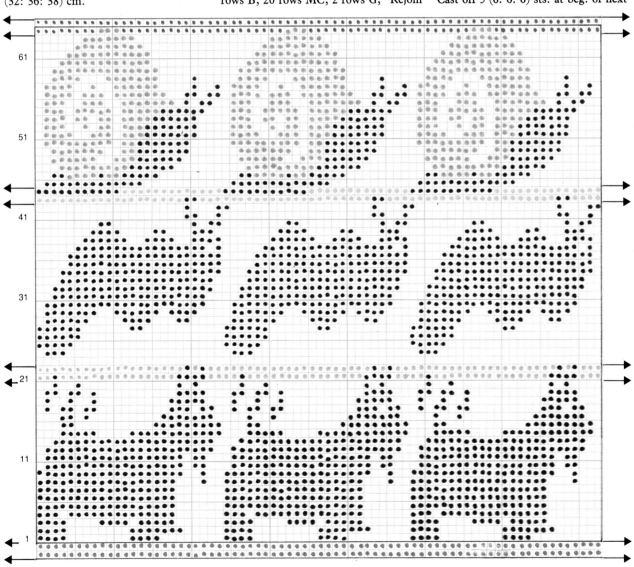

10 (10: 12: 12) rows, and 6 (4: 3: 6) sts. at beg. of next 2 rows.
Leave rem. 40 (42: 42: 44) sts. on a holder.

FRONT

24, 26 in. size.
Work as given for back to★★
28, 30 in. size.
Work as given for back to★★★
ALL SIZES
Commence patt. as follows:
1st row – with MC, K8 (12: 16: 20) sts. K. 1st row of patt. from chart. K to end of row.
2nd row – with MC, P9 (13: 17: 21) sts, P. 2nd row of patt. from chart. P to end of row.

Cont. working rows of patt. from chart as placed, working stripe rows across all sts. of the front. At the same time when work measures same as back to armholes, shape armholes.

○ To shape armholes

Work as given for back. When patt. completed, cont. stripe patt. as worked for back.
At the same time when work measures 14 (14½: 17½: 18½) in, 36 (37: 44: 47) cm. from beg. shape neck.

○ To shape neck

With RS work facing, K40 (43: 49: 51) sts, turn, leave rem. sts. on a spare needle.★★★★ Dec 1 st. at neck edge on next 11 rows. Work straight until length measures same as back to shoulder, ending at armhole edge.

○ To shape shoulder

Cast off 5 (6: 6: 6) sts. at beg. of next and foll. 4 (4: 5: 5) alt. rows. Work 1 row. Cast off 6 (4: 3: 6) sts.
With RS. work facing sl. next 18 (20: 20: 22) sts. onto a holder. Rejoin yarn to next st. and K. to end of row.
Complete to match first side from★★★★ to end.

SLEEVES

With 2¾ mm needles and MC cast on 48 (52: 56: 60) sts. Work 2 in (5 cm) in K2 P2 rib. On the last row inc. 32 (36: 40: 44) sts. evenly. [80 (88: 96: 104) sts].
Change to 3¼ mm needles and starting with a K row, work in st. st. Cont. straight and in stripe patt. as follows.
24/26 in. size.
*20 rows MC, 2 rows E, 20 rows MC, 2 rows F, 20 rows MC, 2 rows B, 20 rows MC, 2 rows G. * Rejoin MC and work 4 (6) rows. Cast off.
28 in. size.
Work as for 24/26 in. size from * to *

Rejoin MC and work 20 rows.★★ Cast off.
30 in. size.
Work as for 28 in. size to ★★. Work 2 rows C, rejoin MC and work 8 rows. Cast off.

NECKBAND

Sew up left shoulder seam. With RS work facing, 2¾ mm needles and MC, pick up and K40 (42: 42: 44) sts. from back neck, 20 (20: 22: 22) sts. from left side neck, 18 (20: 20: 22) sts. from centre front and 20 (20: 22: 22) sts. from right side neck. [98 (102: 106: 110) sts]. Work 2 in (5 cm) in K2 P2 rib. Cast off loosely in rib.

TO MAKE UP

Press work according to yarn instructions, omitting ribbing. Sew up right shoulder and neckband. Fold neckband in half and sew down on wrong side. Sew in sleeves. Sew up side and sleeve seams.

SUGAR AND SPICE...

. . . and all things nice. The sweets can be positioned as you like and the garment can be worn either as a sweater, as shown in the photograph, or as a dress.

MATERIALS

Yarn 4 (4: 6: 8) × 50g 4 ply main colour (pink)
Small amounts of liquorice allsort colours. (White, black, pale blue, yellow, red, brown.)
Needles 1 pair 2¾mm (UK 12) 1 pair 3¼mm (UK 10)

MEASUREMENTS

To fit chest 22 (24: 26: 28) in., 56 (61: 66: 71) cm.
Length 19¼ (20¾: 24: 27) in., 49 (53: 61: 69) cm
Sleeve seam 8½ (10: 12: 14) in., 21 (25: 30: 36) cm

TENSION

28 sts and 36 rows to 10 cm square on 3¼mm needles (or size needed to obtain given tension).

SPECIAL NOTE

Patterns for different liquorice allsorts are included. The individual may choose from these and place them as desired.

BACK

With 2¾mm needles and MC cast on 84 (90: 98: 106) sts. Work 3½ in (9 cm) in K2 P2 rib.
Change to 3¼mm needles and starting with a K row, work in st. st. Cont. straight until work measures 15½ (16½: 19¾: 22) in, 39 (42: 50: 56) cm from beg. ending with a P row.

○ To shape armholes
Inc. 1 st. at both ends of next and every foll. 10th row 4 (5: 5: 6) times. [94 (102: 110: 120) sts]. Work 9 (3: 3: 5) rows straight.

○ To shape shoulders
Cast off 6 (5: 6: 6) sts. at beg. of next

The pink line round the white sweets indicates the edge of the background colour.

8 (10: 10: 12) rows, and 4 (6: 4: 3) sts. at beg. of next 2 rows.
Leave rem. 38 (40: 42: 42) sts. on a holder.

FRONT

Work as given for back until work measures 19 (20½: 23¾: 26¾) in, 48 (52: 60: 68) cm. from beg. Shape neck.

○ To shape neck
With RS work facing K 37 (41: 44: 49) sts, turn, leave rem. sts. on a spare needle. *Dec 1 st. at neck edge on the next 10 rows. Work straight until length measures same as back to shoulder, ending at armhole edge.

○ To shape shoulder
Cast off 6 (5: 6: 6) sts. at beg. of next and foll. 3 (4: 4: 5) alt. rows. Work 1

row.
Cast off 4 (6: 4: 3) sts.
With RS work facing sl. next 18 (20: 22: 22) sts onto a holder. Rejoin yarn to next st. and K to end of row.
Complete to match first side from * to end.

SLEEVES

With 2¾mm needles and MC cast on 46 (50: 50: 56) sts. Work 2 in (5 cm) in K2 P2 rib. On the last row inc. 32 (34: 34: 42) sts evenly. [78 (84: 84: 98) sts].
Change to 3¼mm needles and starting with a K row, work in st. st. Cont. straight until work measures 8½ (10: 12: 14) in, 21 (25: 30: 36) cm. from beg. Cast off.

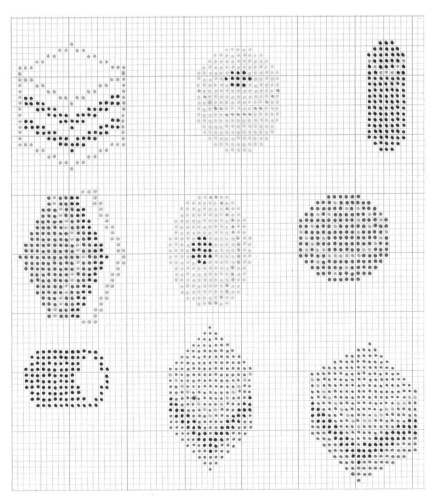

NECKBAND

Sew up left shoulder seam. With RS work facing, 2¾mm needles and MC, pick up and K 38 (40: 42: 42) sts. from back neck, 20 sts. from left side neck, 18 (20: 22: 22) sts. from centre front and 20 sts. from right side neck. [96 (100: 104: 104) sts]. Work 2 in (5 cm) in K2 P2 rib. Cast off loosely in rib.

TO MAKE UP

Press work according to yarn instructions, omitting ribbing. Sew up right shoulder and neckband. Fold neckband in half and sew down on wrong side. Sew in sleeves. Sew up side and sleeve seams. Fold lower edge of dress in half and hem cast on edge to wrong side of work.

READY, TEDDY, GO!

A jumper featuring everybody's favourite toy – the teddy bear.

MATERIALS

Yarn 4 (5: 5) × 50g balls 4 ply in main colour (blue)
Small amount Contrast A – sand, Contrast B – red, Contrast C – fuchsia, Contrast D – black.
Needles 1 pair 2¾mm (UK 12)
1 pair 3¼mm (UK 10)

MEASUREMENTS

To fit chest 24 (26: 28) in, 61 (66: 71) cm
Length 16 (16½: 17½) in, 41 (42: 44) cm
Sleeve seam 11½ (12½: 13½) in, 29 (32: 34) cm

TENSION

28 sts and 36 rows to 10 cm square on 3¼mm needles (or size needed to obtain given tension).

BACK

With 2¾mm needles cast on 90 (98: 106) sts. Work in K2 P2 rib for 4 cms. Change to 3¼mm needles and starting with a K row, work in st. st. Cont. straight until work measures 10 (10½: 11½) in, 26 (27: 29) cm. from beg, ending with a P row.

○ To shape armholes
Inc 1 st. at both ends of next and every foll. 10th row, 5 times, [102 (110: 118) sts]. Work 3 rows straight.

○ To shape shoulders
Cast off 5 (6: 6) sts at beg. of next 10 rows, and 6 (4: 7) sts. at beg. of next 2 rows.
Leave rem. 40 (42: 44) sts on a holder.

FRONT

Work as given for back until work measures 2½ (2¾: 3½) in., 6 (7: 9) cm. from beg. ending with a P row.
Next row – K10 (14: 18) sts, K 1st row of patt. from chart, K to end of row.
Next row – P11 (15: 19) sts. P 2nd row of patt. from chart, P to end of row.
Cont. working rows of patt. from chart as placed. At the same time when work measures same as back to armholes, shape armholes.

○ To shape armholes
Work as for back. At the same time when work measures 14 (14½: 15½) in, 36 (37: 39) cm from beg. shape neck.

○ To shape neck
With RS work facing, K 40 (43: 46) sts, turn, leave rem. sts on a spare needle. ★
Dec. 1 st. at neck edge on the next 11 rows. Work straight until length measures same as back to shoulder, ending at armhole edge.

○ To shape shoulder
Cast off 5 (6: 6) sts at beg. of next and foll. 4 alt. rows.
Work 1 row. Cast off 6 (4: 7) sts.
With RS work facing, slip next 18 (20: 22) sts onto a holder. Rejoin yarn to next st. and K to end.
Complete to match first side from ★ to end.

SLEEVES

With 2¾mm needles cast on 48 (52: 54) sts. Work in K2 P2 rib for 2 in. (5 cm). On the last row inc. 32 sts evenly [80 (84: 86) sts].
Change to 3¼mm needles and starting with a K row, work in st. st. Cont. straight until work measures 11½ (12½: 13½) in, 29 (32: 34) cm. from beg. Cast off.

NECKBAND

Sew up left shoulder seam. With RS facing and 2¾mm needles pick up and K 40 (42: 44) sts from back neck, 20 sts from left side neck, 18 (20: 22) sts from centre front and 20 sts from right side neck [98 (102: 106) sts].
Work in K2 P2 rib for 1¾ in. (4 cm). Cast off loosely in rib.

TO MAKE UP

Press work according to yarn instructions, omitting ribbing.
Sew up right shoulder and neckband. Fold neckband in half and sew down on wrong side. Sew in sleeves. Sew up side and sleeve seams.

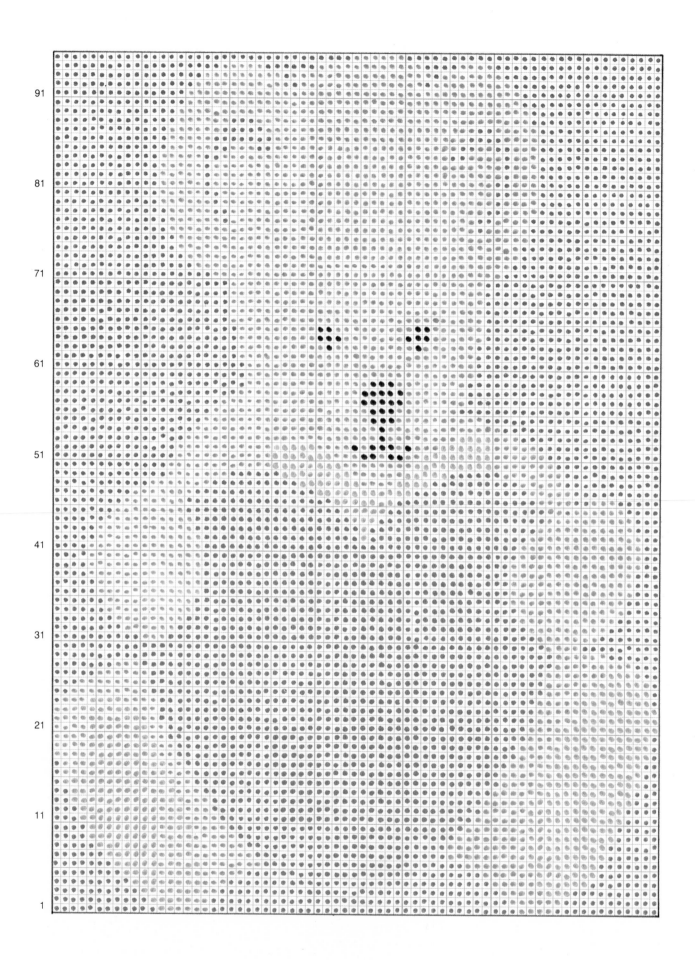

91

81

71

61

51

41

31

21

11

1

24

TOUGH GUY

A zip-up jacket that's as tough as its wearer.

MATERIALS

Yarn 3 (3: 4: 4) × 50g 4 ply main colour (grey)
2 (2: 3: 3) × 50g contrast A (black)
1 × 50g contrast B (yellow)
Needles 1 pair 2¾mm (UK 12)
1 pair 3¼mm (UK 10)
1 open-ended zipper to fit front.

MEASUREMENTS

To fit chest 24 (26: 28: 30) in, 61 (66: 71: 76) cm
Length 16½ (17½: 19½: 20½) in, 42 (44: 49: 52) cm
Sleeve seam 11½ (12½: 15: 16) in, 29 (32: 38: 41) cm

TENSION

28 sts and 36 rows to 10 cm square on 3¼mm needles (or size needed to obtain given tension).

BACK

With 2¾mm needles and MC cast on 90 (98: 106: 114) sts.
★ Work in K2 P2 rib for 2 in (5 cm). Change to 3¼mm needles and starting with a K row, work in st. st. Cont. straight until work measures 9½ (10: 11½: 12½) in, 24 (25: 29: 32) cm from beg. ending with a P row. Break off MC. Work 2 rows con B. ★ Break off con B and work 8 rows con A. Cont. in con A as follows.

○ To shape armholes and commence patt.

Next row – K1, inc. 1 in next st. K15 (19: 23: 27) sts, K 1st row of patt. from chart, K to last 2 sts inc. 1 in next st. K1.
Next row – P18 (22: 26: 30) sts, P 2nd row of patt. from chart, P to end of row.
Next row – K18 (22: 26: 30) sts, K 3rd row of patt. from chart, K to end of row.
Cont. working rows of patt. from chart as placed. At the same time inc. 1 st. at both ends on the 11th row of patt. then every foll. 10th row until 102 (110: 120: 128) sts.
Work 3 (3: 5: 5) rows straight.

○ To shape shoulders

Cast off 5 (6: 6: 6) sts at beg. of next 10 (10: 12: 12) rows, and 6 (4: 3: 6) sts at beg. of next 2 rows.
Leave rem. 40 (42: 42: 44) sts on a holder.

RIGHT FRONT

With 2¾mm needles and MC cast on 46 (50: 54: 58) sts.
Work as for back from ★ to ★.
Break off con B and complete in con A as follows.
Work 8 rows.

○ To shape armhole

Inc. 1 st. (one st. in), at the end of next and every foll. 10th row 5 (5: 6: 6) times.
At the same time when work measures 14½ (15: 16½: 17½) in., 37 (38: 42: 44) cm from beg. ending with a P row, shape neck.

○ To shape neck

With RS work facing cast off 9 (10: 11: 11) sts. K to end of row.
Dec 1 st. at neck edge on the next 11 rows. Work straight until length measures same as back to shoulder, ending at armhole edge.

○ To shape shoulder

Cast off 5 (6: 6: 6) sts at beg. of next and foll. 4 (4: 5: 5) alt. rows. Work 1 row. Cast off 6 (4: 3: 6) sts.

LEFT FRONT

Work as given for Right Front, reversing all shapings and working own initial if preferred, on the front. (See the Do-It-Yourself Alphabet on page 93) Position the letter over middle sts of the front and commencing on the 9th row after the yellow stripe.

SLEEVES

With 2¾mm needles and MC cast on 48 (52: 56: 60) sts.
Work in K2 P2 rib for 2½ in (6 cm).
On the last row inc. 32 (36: 40: 44) sts. evenly [80 (88: 96: 104) sts].
Change to 3¼mm needles and starting with a K row, work in st. st. Cont. straight until work measures 11 (12: 14½: 15½) in, 28 (30: 37: 39) cm. from beg. ending with a P row. Break off MC, work 2 rows con B and 2 rows con A. Cast off.

PATCH POCKETS

(Work 2)
With 3¼mm needles and con A cast on

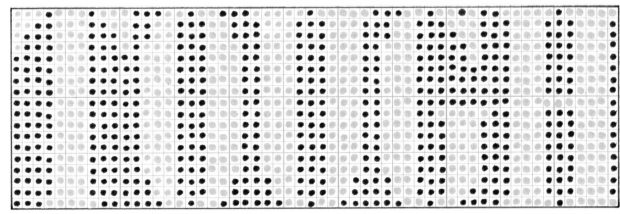

11

1

30 (30: 34: 34) sts.
Starting with a K row, work 3 (3: 4: 4) in, 7.5 (7.5: 10: 10) cm in st. st ending with a P row.
Change to 2¾mm needles and work 6 rows in K2, P2 rib.
Break off con A and work a further 2 rows in con B.
Cast off loosely in rib.

NECKBAND

Join shoulder seams. With RS facing, 2¾mm needles and con A pick up and K 9 (10: 11: 11) sts from right front neck, 20 sts up right side neck, 40 (42: 42: 44) sts from back neck, 20 sts down left side neck and 9 (10: 11: 11) sts from left front neck [98 (102: 104: 106) sts]. Working in K2 P2 rib, work 1 row

con A, 2 rows con B and 15 rows MC. Cast off loosely in rib.

TO MAKE UP

Press work according to yarn instructions omitting ribbing. Fold neckband in half and sew down on wrong side. Sew in sleeves, sew up side and sleeve seams. Sew on patch pockets. Insert zip.

BOSSY BOOTS

This smart polo-necked sweater leaves no doubts as to who is in charge!

MATERIALS

Yarn 3 (3: 4: 4) × 50g 4 ply main colour (black)
3 (3: 4: 4) × 50g Contrast A (red)
1 × 50g Contrast B (yellow)
Needles 1 pair 2¾mm (UK 12)
1 pair 3¼mm (UK 10)

MEASUREMENTS

To fit chest 24 (26: 28: 30) in, 61 (66: 71: 76) cm
Length 16 (16½: 19½: 20½) in, 41 (42: 49: 52) cm
Sleeve seam 11½ (12½: 15: 16) in, 29 (32: 38: 41) cm

TENSION

28 sts and 36 rows to 10 cm square on 3¼mm needles (or size needed to obtain given tension).

BACK

With 2¾mm needles and MC cast on 90 (98: 106: 114) sts.
Working in K2 P2 rib, work 1 in. (2.5 cm) MC, 3 rows con B, then 1 in. (2.5 cm) MC.
Change to 3¼mm needles and starting with a K row, work in st. st. Cont. straight until work measures 10 (10½: 12½: 13½) in, 25 (27: 32: 34) cm from beg. ending with a P row.

○ To shape armholes
Inc. 1 st. at both ends of next and every foll. 10th row 5 (5: 6: 6) times. [102 (110: 120: 128) sts].
Work 3 (3: 5: 5) rows straight.

○ To shape shoulders
Cast off 5 (6: 6: 6) sts at beg. of next 10 (10: 12: 12) rows, and 6 (4: 3: 6) sts at beg. of next 2 rows.
Leave rem. 40 (42: 42: 44) sts on a holder.

FRONT

Work as given for back until work measures 6 (6½: 8½: 9½) in, 15 (16: 21: 24) cm from beg. ending with a P row.
Next row – K20 (24: 28: 32) sts, K 1st

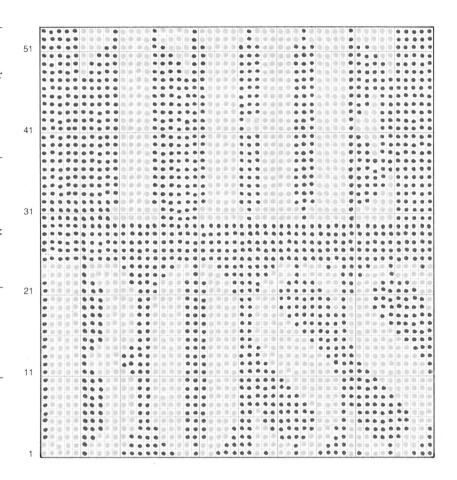

row of patt. from chart, K to end of row.
Next row – P20 (24: 28: 32) sts, P 2nd row of patt. from chart, P to end of row.
Cont. working rows of patt. from chart as placed. At the same time when work measures same as back to armholes, shape armholes.

○ To shape armholes
Work as for back. At the same time when work measures 14 (14½: 17½: 18½) in, 36 (37: 44: 47) cm from beg, shape neck.

○ To shape neck
With RS work facing, K40 (43: 49: 51) sts, turn, leave rem. sts on a spare needle. * Dec. 1 st. at neck edge on the next 11 rows. Work straight until length measures same as back to shoulder, ending at armhole edge.

○ To shape shoulder
Cast off 5 (6: 6: 6) sts at beg. of next

and foll. 4 (4: 5: 5) alt. rows. Work 1 row. Cast off 6 (4: 3: 6) sts.
With RS facing slip next 18 (20: 20: 22) sts onto a holder.
Rejoin yarn to next st. and K to end of row.
Complete to match first side from * to end.

SLEEVES

With 2¾mm needles and con A cast on 48 (52: 56: 60) sts.
Working in K2 P2 rib work 1¼ in (3 cm) con A, 3 rows con B, then 1¼ in. (3 cm) con A. On the last row inc. 32 (36: 40: 44) sts evenly. [80 (88: 96: 104) sts].
Cont. in con A, change to 3¼mm needles and starting with a K row work in st. st. Cont. straight until work measures 10¾ (11¾: 14¼: 15¼) in, 27 (30: 36: 39) cm from beg. Break off con A. Work 3 rows con B, then 3 rows MC. Cast off.

POLO COLLAR

Sew up left shoulder seam.
With RS work facing, con A and
2¾mm needles, pick up and K 40 (42:
42: 44) sts from back neck, 20 sts from
left side neck, 18 (20: 20: 22) sts from
centre front, and 20 sts from right side
neck. [98 (102: 102: 106) sts]. Work in
K2 P2 rib for 4½ in (11 cm).

Break off con A, work 4 rows con B.
Cast off loosely in rib.

TO MAKE UP

Press work according to yarn
instructions, omitting ribbing. Sew up
right shoulder and polo collar. Sew in
sleeves. Sew up side and sleeve seams.

WORK WEAR

These dungarees for a little boy or girl can be worked with the initials of your choice (see the alphabet on page 93).

MATERIALS

Yarn 3 (3: 4: 4) × 50g 4 ply main colour (blue)
1 × 50g Contrast A (red)
Small amount Contrast B – (yellow)
4 buttons
Elastic for back waist.
Needles 1 pair 2¾mm (UK 12)
1 pair 3¼mm (UK 10)

MEASUREMENTS

To fit chest 20 (22: 24) in, 51 (56: 61) cm
Hips 24 (26: 28) in, 61 (66: 71) cm finished measurements
Length (waist to bottom of leg) 16½ (17¾: 19¾) in, 42 (45: 50) cm

TENSION

28 sts and 36 rows to 10 cm square on 3¼mm needles (or size needed to obtain given tension).

FRONT

** With 3¼mm needles and MC cast on 38 (42: 45) sts. Starting with a K row, work 9 rows in st. st.
Next row – K (to make fold line for hem).
Beg. with a K row, cont. in st. st. until leg measures 8¼ (9½: 10½) in, 21 (24: 27) cm from fold line for hem, ending with a P row ** Cast on 8 sts, and leave sts on a spare needle.
Work a second leg to match from ** to **
Join legs together as follows.
Next row – K38 (42: 45) sts from 2nd leg, K8 cast on sts, and K 38 (42: 45) sts from 1st leg. [84 (92: 98) sts].
Work straight and in st. st. until legs measure 16½ (17¾: 19¾) in, 42 (45: 50) cm from fold line for hem, ending with a P row. ***

◯ To shape front

Cast off 10 sts at beg. of next 2 rows and 3 sts at beg. of foll. 2 rows. Dec. 1 st. at both ends of next 8 rows. [42 (50: 56) sts].
Cont. in st. st and without further shaping, work 30 more rows.
Cast off.

BACK

Work as given for front from ** to ***

◯ To shape back

1st row – K to last 5 (5: 6) sts, turn.
2nd row – P to last 5 (5: 6) sts, turn.
Rep. last 2 rows 3 times more, leaving 5 (5: 6) sts unworked at end of each row.
Work 4 more rows leaving 6 (7: 7) sts unworked at end of each row.
Leave rem. 20 (24: 22) sts on a spare needle.
With RS work facing rejoin yarn to first set of sts. at beg. of shaping and K across all sts.
Work 11 more rows in st. st. Cast off.

POCKETS

Plain pocket (make 1)
With 3¼mm needles and MC cast on 28 (32: 35) sts.*
Starting with a K row work 3¼ (3¾: 4) in, 8 (9: 10) cm in st. st. ** Change to 2¾mm needles and work 2 in (5 cm) in st. st. Cast off.

Pockets with initials (make 2)
Work as for plain pocket to *. Starting with a K row, work 6 rows in st. st.
Join in con A and work 3 rows more.
Work 1 row MC. Over the next 18 rows:
Work own initials from patts. as given for the Tough Guy jacket (page 25) in con A.
When initials completed, work 1 row MC then 3 rows con A.
Rejoin MC and cont. until work measures 3¼ (3¾: 4) in, 8 (9: 10) cm from beg. Complete as for plain pocket from ** to end.

STRAPS

(Make 2)
With 2¾mm needles and MC cast on 10 sts. Work in garter st. for 14 in (36 cm) or required length. Cast off.

TO MAKE UP

Press work according to yarn instructions, omitting straps.

Sew up side and leg seams. Fold lower edge of legs along fold line and hem cast on edge to wrong side.
Fold over ¾ in (2 cm) along back, sides and top edge of dungarees and sew down on wrong side.
Fold over 1 in (2.5 cm) along pocket top edges and sew down on wrong side.
Sew pockets in place as shown in photograph.
Sew straps in place on back edge. Make 2 buttonloops on top edge of the front. Sew on buttons. Thread elastic through back.
Top-stitch dungarees in cons. A and B. as shown in the photograph.

DOWN ON THE FARM

The next three designs will appeal to all animal lovers. First, a happy duck, on a garment which can either be worn as a sweater, as shown, or as a dress.

MATERIALS

Yarn 4 (5: 7: 9) × 50g 4 ply main colour (red)
1 × 50g Contrast A (yellow)
1 × 50g Contrast B (white)
Small amount Contrast C – black, D – blue.
Needles 1 pair 2¾mm (UK 12)
1 pair 3¼mm (UK 10)

MEASUREMENTS

To fit chest 23 (25: 26: 28) in, 58 (63: 66: 71) cm.
Length 19¼ (22½: 24¼: 27) in, 49 (57: 62: 69) cm
Sleeve seam 8½ (10: 12: 13) in, 22 (25: 30: 33) cm

TENSION

28 sts and 36 rows to 10 cm square on 3¼mm needles (or size needed to obtain given tension).

BACK

With 2¾mm needles and MC cast on 84 (90: 90: 96) sts.
Work 1¼ in (3 cm) in K2 P2 rib. On the last row inc. 16 (18: 18: 20) sts evenly. [100 (108: 108: 116) sts].
Change to 3¼mm needles and starting with a K row, work in st. st. Cont straight until work measures 13¾ (16½: 18: 20½) in, 35 (42: 46: 52) cm from beg. ending with a P row.

○ To shape armholes
** Cast off 3 sts at beg. of next 2 rows.
Cast off 2 sts at beg. of next 2 rows.
Cast off 1 st. at beg. of next 4 rows. [86 (94: 94: 102) sts]. **
Work straight until work measures 19¾ (23: 24¾: 27½) in, 50 (58: 63: 70) cm from beg. ending with a P row.

○ To shape shoulders and neck
Cast off 6 (7: 7: 8) sts at beg. of next 2 (4: 4: 4) rows.
Cast off 7 (0: 0: 0) sts at beg. of next 2 (0: 0: 0) rows.
* *Next row* – Cast off 7 (7: 7: 8) sts., K 7 (8: 8: 8) sts (including st. on needle after cast off), turn, leave rem. sts on a spare needle.

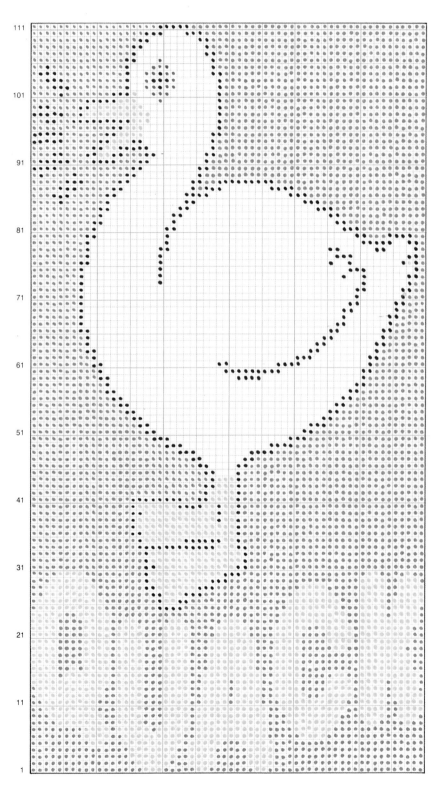

Work 1 row. Cast off 7 (8: 8: 8) sts.
With RS facing, sl. next 32 (36: 36: 38) sts. onto a holder. Rejoin yarn to next st. and K to end of row. Complete to match first side from * to end.

FRONT

Work as given for back until work measures 3½ (6½: 8½: 11) in, 9 (17: 22: 28) cm from beg. ending with a P row.

Next row – K20 (24: 24: 28) sts, K 1st row of patt. from chart, K to end of row.

Next row – P20 (24: 24: 28) sts, P 2nd row of patt. from chart, P to end of row.

Cont. working rows of patt. from chart as placed.

At the same time when work measures same as back to armholes, shape armholes.

○ **To shape armholes**

Work as given for back from ** to ** keeping patt. over central sts as set, work straight until work measures 18 (21: 23: 25½) in, 46 (54: 59: 65) cm from beg.

○ **To shape neck**

With RS work facing K39 (42: 42: 45) sts, turn, leave rem. sts on a spare needle. *** Cast off at neck edge on next and foll. alt. rows 4 sts once, 3 sts once, 2 sts twice and 1 st. 1 (2: 2: 2) times.

Work straight until length measures same as back to shoulder, ending at armhole edge.

○ **To shape shoulder**

Cast off 6 (7: 7: 8) sts at beg. of next row.

Work 1 row.

Cast off 7 (7: 7: 8) sts at beg. of next and foll. alt. row.

Work 1 row.

Cast off 7 (8: 8: 8) sts.

With RS facing sl. next 8. (10: 10: 12) sts onto a holder, rejoin yarn to next st. and complete to match first side from *** to end.

SLEEVES

With 2¾mm needles and MC cast on 44 (44: 44: 48) sts.

Work 2 in (5 cm) in K2 P2 rib. On the last row inc. 16 sts evenly [60: (60: 60: 64 sts].

Change to 3¼mm needles, and starting with a K row, work in st. st. At the same time inc. 1 st. at both ends of every 4th row until 94 (98: 98: 104) sts.

Work straight until sleeve measures 8½ (10: 12: 13) in, 22 (25: 30: 33) cm from beg. ending with a P row.

○ **To shape top**

Cast off 7 (7: 7: 8) sts at beg. of next 6 rows and 7 (9: 9: 8) sts at beg. of next 2 rows.

Cast off rem 38 (38: 38: 40) sts.

NECKBAND

Sew up left shoulder seam.

With RS facing and 2¾mm needles, pick up and K3 sts down right back neck, 32 (36: 36: 38) sts from back neck, 3 sts up left back neck, 20 (20: 20: 21) sts. from left front neck, 9 (10: 10: 12) sts from centre front and 19 (20: 20: 21) sts from right front neck. [86 (92: 92: 98) sts]. Work 2 in (5 cm) in K2, P2, rib. Cast off loosely in rib.

TO MAKE UP

Press work according to yarn instructions, omitting ribbing.

Sew up right shoulder and neckband. Fold neckband in half and sew down on wrong side.

Sew in sleeves. Sew up side and sleeve seams.

Fold cuffs and lower edge of dress in half and hem cast on edges to wrong side of work.

GUARD DOG

The second farmyard sweater features a bouncy dog.

MATERIALS

Yarn 4 (5: 5: 6) × 50g balls 4 ply in main colour (yellow)
1 × 50g Contrast A and B (blue and white)
Small amounts Contrast C – black, D – red.
Needles 1 pair 2¾mm (UK 12)
1 pair 3¼mm (UK 10)

MEASUREMENTS

To fit chest 24 (26: 28: 30) in, 61 (66: 71: 76) cm
Length 16 (16½: 19½: 20½) in, 41 (42: 49: 52) cm
Sleeve seam 11½ (12½: 14: 15) in, 29 (32: 35: 38) cm

TENSION

28 sts and 36 rows to 10 cm square on 3¼mm needles (or size needed to obtain given tension).

BACK

With 2¾mm needles cast on 90 (98: 106: 114) sts. Work in K2, P2 rib for 4 cm. Change to 3¼mm needles and starting with a K row, work in st. st. Cont. straight until work measures 10 (10½: 12½: 13½) in, 26 (27: 32: 34) cm from beg ending with a P row.

○ To shape armholes
Inc. 1 st. at both ends of next and every foll. 10th row 5 (5: 6: 6) times. [102 (110: 120: 128) sts]. Work 3 (3: 5: 5) rows straight.

○ To shape shoulders
Cast off 5 (6: 6: 6) sts. at beg. of next 10 (10: 12: 12) rows, and 6 (4: 3: 6) sts at beg. of next 2 rows.
Leave rem. 40 (42: 42: 44) sts on a holder.

FRONT

Work as given for back until work measures 2 (2½: 4½: 5) in, 5 (6: 11: 13) cm from beg. ending with a P row.
Next row – K11 (15: 19: 23) sts, K 1st row of patt. from chart, K to end of row.
Next row – P12 (16: 20: 24) sts, P 2nd row of patt. from chart, P to end of row.
Cont. working rows of patt. from chart as placed. At the same time when work measures same as back to armholes, shape armholes.

○ To shape armholes
Work as for back. At the same time when work measures 14 (14½: 17½: 18½) in., 36 (37: 44: 47) cm from beg. shape neck.

○ To shape neck
With RS work facing K40 (43: 49: 51) sts, turn, leave rem. sts on a spare needle. ★ Dec. 1 st. at neck edge on the next 11 rows. Work straight until length measures same as back to shoulder, ending at armhole edge.

○ To shape shoulder
Cast off 5 (6: 6: 6) sts at beg. of next and foll. 4 (4: 5: 5) alt. rows. Work 1 row. Cast off 6 (4: 3: 6) sts.
With RS work facing sl. next 18 (20: 22: 22) sts. onto a holder. Rejoin yarn to next st. and K to end of row.
Complete to match first side from ★ to end.

SLEEVES

With 2¾mm needles cast on 48 (52: 56: 60) sts and work in K2, P2 rib for 2 in. (5cm). On the last row inc. 32 (36: 40: 44) sts. evenly. [80 (88: 96: 104) sts].
Change to 3¼mm needles and starting with a K row, work in st. st. Cont. straight until work measures 11½ (12½: 14: 15) in, 29 (32: 36: 38) cm from beg. Cast off.

NECKBAND

Sew up left shoulder seam. With RS work facing and 2¾mm needles, pick up and K40 (42: 42: 44) sts from back neck, 20 (20: 22: 22) sts from left side neck, 18 (20: 22: 22) sts from centre front and 20 (20: 22: 22) sts from right side neck.
[98 (102: 106: 110) sts]. Work in K2, P2 rib for 2 in. (5 cm).
Cast off loosely in rib.

TO MAKE UP

Press work according to yarn instructions, omitting ribbing.
Sew up right shoulder and neckband. Fold neckband in half and sew down on wrong side. Sew in sleeves. Sew up side and sleeve seams.

DAISY, DAISY

And Daisy, the contented cow, is included here in response to the many requests received for a cow pattern.

MATERIALS

Yarn 5 (6: 6: 7) × 50g 4 ply main colour (green)
1 × 50g Contrast A – white
1 × 50g Contrast B – black.
Needles 1 pair 2¾mm (UK 12)
1 pair 3¼mm (UK 10)

MEASUREMENTS

To fit bust/chest 30 (32: 34: 36) in., 76 (81: 87: 92) cm
Length 20½ (21½: 22½: 23½) in., 52 (55: 57: 60) cm

Sleeve seam 16 (17: 18: 19) in., 41 (43: 46: 48) cm

TENSION

28 sts and 36 rows to 10 cm square on 3¼mm needles (or size needed to obtain given tension).

BACK

With 2¾mm needles and MC cast on 114 (120: 126: 132) sts.
** Working in K2, P2, rib work 2 rows MC, 3 rows con A, then 2 in (5 cm) MC. **

Change to 3¼mm needles and starting with a K row, work in st. st. Cont. straight until work measures 13½ (14½: 15½: 16½) in, 34 (37: 39: 42) cm from beg. ending with a P row.

○ **To shape armholes**
Inc. 1 st. at both ends of next and every foll. 10th row, 6 times, [128 (134: 140: 146) sts]. Work 5 rows straight.

○ **To shape shoulders**
Cast off 6 (6: 7: 7) sts at beg. next 12 rows, and 6 (8: 4: 6) sts at beg. of next 2 rows.
Leave rem. 44 (46: 48: 50) sts on a holder.

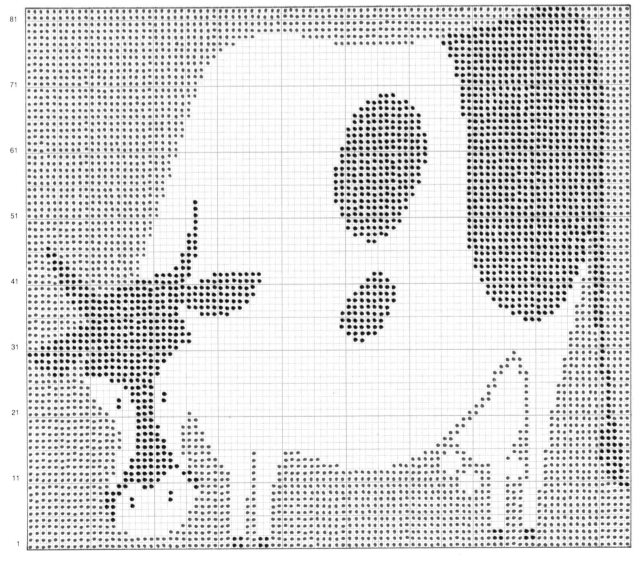

FRONT

Work as given for back until work measures 7½ (8½: 9½: 10½) in, 19 (21: 24: 27) cm from beg. ending with a P row.

Next row – K12 (15: 18: 21) sts, K 1st row of patt. from chart, K to end of row.

Next row – P7 (10: 13: 16) sts, P 2nd row of patt. from chart, P to end of row.

Cont. working rows of patt. from chart as placed. At the same time when work measures same as back to armholes, shape armholes.

○ To shape armholes

Work as for back. At the same time when work measures 18½ (19½: 20½: 21½) in, 47 (49: 52: 55) cm from beg. shape neck.

○ To shape neck

With RS work facing K51 (53: 55: 57) sts, turn, leave rem. sts on a spare needle. * Dec. 1 st. at neck edge on next 11 rows. Work straight until length measures same as back to shoulder, ending at armhole edge.

○ To shape shoulder

Cast off 6 (6: 7: 7) sts at beg. of next and foll. 5 alt. rows.
Work 1 row. Cast off 6 (8: 4: 6) sts.
With RS work facing sl. next 22 (24: 26: 28) sts onto a holder. Rejoin yarn to next st. and K to end of row.
Complete to match first side from * to end.

SLEEVES

With 2¾mm needles and MC cast on 60 (60: 64: 64) sts.
Work as for back from ** to **. On the last row inc. 44 (44: 48: 48) sts evenly. [104 (104: 112: 112) sts].
Change to 3¼mm needles and starting with a K row, work in st. st. Cont. straight until work measures 16 (17: 18: 19) in., 41 (43: 46: 48) cm from beg. Cast off.

NECKBAND

Sew up left shoulder seam.
With 2¾mm needles and MC pick up and K44 (46: 48: 50) sts, from back neck, 22 sts. from left side neck, 22 (24: 26: 28) sts, from centre front and 22 sts from right side neck. [110 (114: 118: 122) sts].
Working in K2 P2 rib, work 6 rows MC, 3 rows con A, and 13 rows MC. Cast off loosely in rib.

TO MAKE UP

Press work according to yarn instructions, omitting ribbing.
Sew up right shoulder and neckband.
Fold neckband in half and sew down on wrong side.
Sew in sleeves. Sew up side and sleeve seams.

PIERRETTE

The circus comes to town with this pretty pierrette outfit – dress, scarf and bag –
based on the traditional clown's costume.

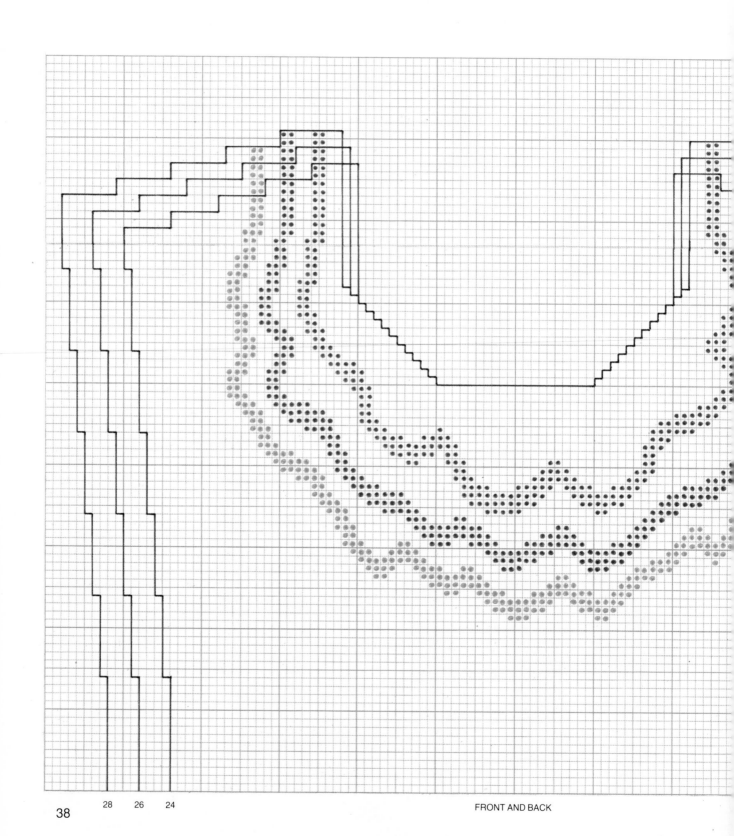

28   26   24

FRONT AND BACK

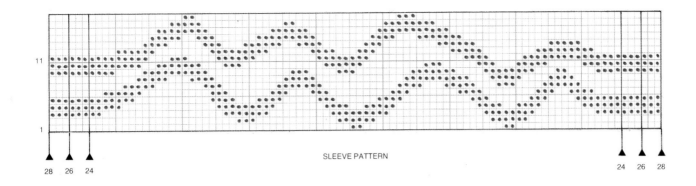

SLEEVE PATTERN

28   26   24   24   26   28

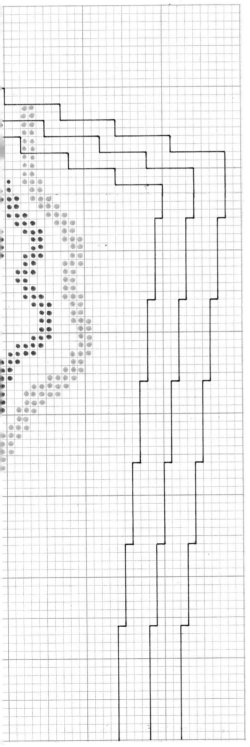

24   26   28

DRESS

MATERIALS

Yarn 4 (5: 7) × 50g 4 ply main colour
(white)
1 × 50g Contrast A (grey)
1 × 50g Contrast B (fuchsia)
Needles 1 pair 2¾mm (UK 12)
1 pair 3¼mm (UK 10)

MEASUREMENTS

To fit chest 24 (26: 28) in, 61 (66: 71)
cm
Length 19 (21¼: 24) in, 48 (54: 61) cm
Sleeve seam 10½ (12½: 14) in, 26 (31:
36) cm

TENSION

28 sts and 36 rows to 10 cm square on
3¼mm needles, (or size needed to
obtain given tension).

BACK

Frill
With 2¾mm needles and MC cast on
176 (192: 208) sts.
Starting with a K row, work in st. st.
Work 4 rows MC, then 3 rows con A.
Cont. in con A and K 1 row, to make
fold line for hem. Cont. in st. st. and
work 3 more rows con A.
Rejoin MC and work 5 rows. Change to
3¼mm needles and work 10 rows.
Rejoin con A and work 3 rows.
Rejoin MC and work a further 2¼ in.
(6 cm), ending with a K row.
Next row – * P2tog, rep. from * to end.
[88 (96: 104) sts].

Main body
Starting with a K row, work in st. st.
Cont. straight until work measures 8½
(10½: 13) in., 22 (27: 33) cm. from beg.
of main body, ending with a P row.

○ To shape armholes
Inc. 1 st. at both ends of next and every

foll. 10th row 5 times [100 (108: 116)
sts]. Work 3 (5: 7) rows straight.
At the same time work patt. from chart
as given for front of dress, commencing
after the first inc., as shown**.

○ To shape shoulders
Cast off 6 (6: 7) sts at beg. of next 4
rows, 6 (7: 7) sts. at beg of next 4 rows,
and 6 (7: 8) sts at beg. of next 2 rows.
Leave rem. 40 (42: 44) sts on a holder.

FRONT

Work as given for back to ** At the
same time, when work measures 12½
(14½: 17) in., 32 (37: 43) cm from beg.
of main body, shape neck.

○ To shape neck
With RS work facing patt. 38 (42: 46)
sts, turn, leave rem. sts on a spare
needle. *** Dec. 1 st. at neck edge on
the next 10 (11: 12) rows. Work
straight until length measures same as
back to shoulder, ending at armhole
edge.

○ To shape shoulder
Cast off 6 (6: 7) sts at beg. of next and
foll. alt. row.
Work 1 row. Cast off 6 (7: 7) sts at beg.
of next and foll. alt. row. Work 1 row.
Cast off 6 (7: 8) sts.
With RS work facing sl. next 20 sts onto
a holder. Rejoin yarn to next st. and
patt. to end of row.
Complete to match first side from ***
to end.

SLEEVES

With 2¾mm needles and MC cast on
50 (54: 58) sts.
Work 2 in (5 cm) in K2 P2 rib. On the
last row inc. 30 (32: 34) sts evenly [80
(86: 92) sts].
Change to 3¼mm needles and starting
with a K row, work in st. st. Work 4
rows in MC. Join in con A and work
patt. from chart as given for sleeves.
When patt. completed, cont. straight
and in MC until work measures 10½
(12½: 14) in, 26 (31: 36) cm from beg.
Cast off.

39

NECKBAND

Sew up left shoulder seam. With RS work facing, 2¾mm needles and MC, pick up and K40 (42: 44) sts from back neck, 20 (22: 24) sts from left side neck, 20 sts from centre front and 20 (22: 24) sts from right side neck. [100 (106: 112) sts] Work 2 in (5 cm) in K2 P2 rib. Cast off loosely in rib.

TO MAKE UP

Press work according to yarn instructions, omitting ribbing.
Sew up right shoulder and neckband. Fold neckband in half and sew down on wrong side. Sew in sleeves. Sew up side, frill and sleeves seams. Fold lower edge of dress along fold line and hem cast on edge to wrong side of work.
Make 5 pompons in con B and sew on dress as shown in photograph.

SCARF

MATERIALS

Yarn 2 × 50g 4 ply main colour (white)
1 × 50g Contrast A (grey)
1 × 50g Contrast B (fuchsia)
Needles 1 pair 3¼mm (UK 10)

MEASUREMENTS

Length 24 in, 61 cm
Width 5½ in, 14 cm

INSTRUCTIONS

With 3¼mm needles and MC cast on 80 sts. Starting with a K row, work 2 in (5 cm) in st. st. Join in con A and work rows of patt. as given for sleeves, starting and finishing where indicated for 24 in (61 cm) size.
When patt. completed work a further 16 in (41 cm) in MC.
Join in con A and rep. patt. rows again. When patt. completed break off con A and work a further 2 in (5 cm) in MC. Cast off.

TO MAKE UP

Press work according to yarn instructions. Join long edge together and placing seam at centre back, press again.
Make 2 pompons in con A and 4 pompons in con B.
Gather ends of scarf together and sew on pompons as shown in photograph.

BAG

MATERIALS

Yarn 1 × 50g 4 ply main colour (white)
Small amounts con A – grey, con B – fuchsia
Needles 1 pair 3¼mm (UK 10)

MEASUREMENTS

9 in × 4½ in (approx) 23 × 12 cm

INSTRUCTIONS

With 3¼mm needles and MC cast on 64 sts. * Working in K2 P2 rib, work 8 rows MC, 7 rows con A and 8 rows MC. * Cont. in MC and starting with a K row, work 6½ in (17 cm) in st. st. Rep. from * to * once. Cast off loosely in rib.

TO MAKE UP

Press work according to yarn instructions, omitting ribbing.
Fold top and bottom ribbing in half and sew down on wrong side, leaving ends open.

Fold work in half and sew up side seams to ribbing.
Make a draw string using 4 strands MC twisted together, and thread through ribbing.
Make 2 pompons in con A, and 2 pompons in con B. Sew on bag as shown in photograph.

PRANCING PONY

Continuing the circus theme, a prancing white pony decorates this tunic-style sweater.

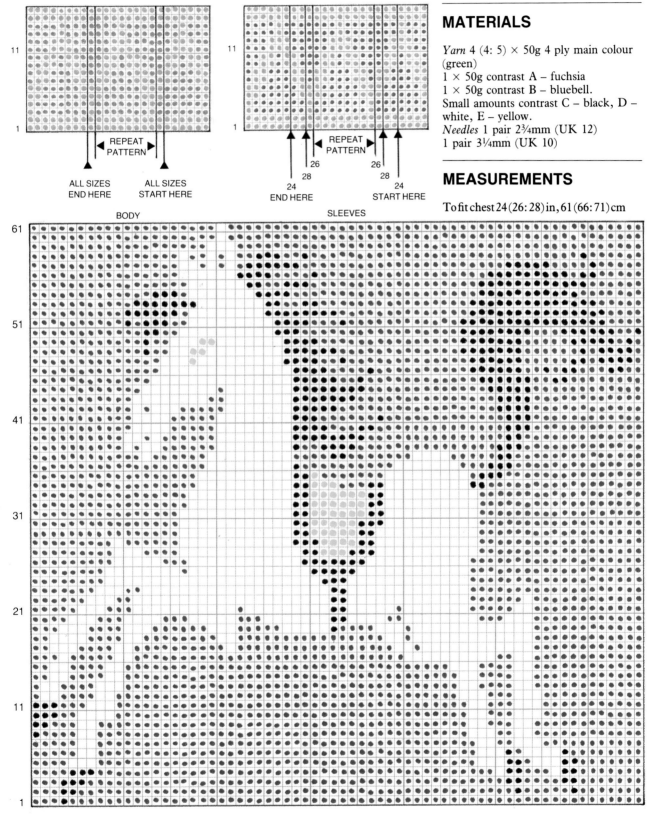

BODY

SLEEVES

MATERIALS

Yarn 4 (4: 5) × 50g 4 ply main colour
(green)
1 × 50g contrast A – fuchsia
1 × 50g contrast B – bluebell.
Small amounts contrast C – black, D –
white, E – yellow.
Needles 1 pair 2¾mm (UK 12)
1 pair 3¼mm (UK 10)

MEASUREMENTS

To fit chest 24(26: 28) in, 61 (66: 71) cm

Length 16 (16½: 17½) in, 41 (42: 44) cm
Sleeve seam 10½ (11½: 12½) in, 27 (29: 32) cm

TENSION

28 sts and 36 rows to 10 cm square on 3¼mm needles (or size needed to obtain given tension).

BACK

With 2¾mm needles and MC cast on 90 (98: 106) sts.
** Starting with a K row, work 17 rows in st. st, then K 1 row to make fold line for hem.
Cont. in st. st. and work 2 rows MC. Joining in contrasts where necessary work rows of zig-zag patt. from chart. across all sts, in st. st.
When patt. completed, change to 3¼mm needles and rejoin MC. **
Cont. straight and in st. st until work measures 10 (10½: 11½) in, 26 (27: 29) cm from fold line for hem, ending with a P row.

○ To shape armholes
Inc. 1 st. at both ends of next and every foll. 10th row 5 times. [102 (110: 118) sts]. Work 3 rows straight.

○ To shape shoulders
Cast off 5 (6: 6) sts at beg. of next 10 rows, and 6 (4: 7) sts. at beg. of next 2 rows.
Leave rem. 40 (42: 44) sts on a holder.

FRONT

Work as given for back until work measures 5 (5½: 6½) in, 13 (14: 16) cm from fold line for hem, ending with a P row.
Next row – K12 (16: 20) sts, K 1st row of patt 2 from chart, K to end of row.
Next row – P12 (16: 20) sts, P 2nd row of patt. 2 from chart, P to end of row.
Cont. working rows of patt. 2 from chart as placed.
At the same time when work measures same as back to armholes, shape armholes.

○ To shape armholes
Work as for back. At the same time when work measures 14 (14½: 15½) in, 36 (37: 39) cm from fold line for hem, shape neck.

○ To shape neck
With RS work facing, K40 (43: 46) sts, turn, leave rem. sts on a spare needle. * Dec. 1 st. at neck edge on the next 11 rows. Work straight until length

measures same as back to shoulder, ending at armhole edge.

○ To shape shoulder
Cast off 5 (6: 6) sts at beg. of next and foll. 4 alt. rows. Work 1 row. Cast off 6 (4: 7) sts.
With RS work facing, sl. next 18 (20: 22) sts. onto a holder. Rejoin yarn to next st. and K to end.
Complete to match first side from * to end.

SLEEVES

With 2¾mm needles and MC cast on 62 (64: 66) sts.
Work as given for back from ** to **.
Cont. in st. st. and at the same time inc. 1 st. at both ends on the 7th row and then every foll. 6th row to 78 (80: 82) sts.
Work straight until sleeve measures 10½ (11½: 12½) in, 27 (29: 32) cm from fold line for hem, ending with a P row.
Cast off.

NECKBAND

Sew up left shoulder seam. With RS facing, MC and 2¾mm needles pick up and K40 (42: 44) sts from back neck, 20 (22: 20) sts from left side neck, 18 (20: 22) sts. from centre front and 20 (22: 20) sts from right side neck. [98 (106: 106) sts].
Next row – Purl.
Joining in contrasts where necessary work rows of zig-zag patt. from chart in st. st., starting and ending as indicated for body.
When patt. completed rejoin MC and work 22 rows in st. st. Cast off loosely.

TO MAKE UP

Press work according to yarn instructions. Sew up right shoulder and neckband. Fold neckband in half and sew down on wrong side. Sew in sleeves. Sew up side and sleeve seams. Slip stitch hem and bottoms of sleeves up on wrong side.

COLOURFUL CLASSICS

The next five patterns feature vividly coloured modern variations on a traditional theme.
First, a wonderfully warm Aran dress with a bag and hat to match . . .

DRESS

MATERIALS

Yarn – 7 (8: 9: 10) × 50g Pingouin Orage
Needles 1 pair 3¾mm (UK 9)
1 pair 4½mm (UK 7)
1 cable needle.

MEASUREMENTS

To fit chest 24 (26: 28: 30) in, 61 (66: 71: 76) cm
Length 22 (24: 26¾: 30½) in, 56 (61: 68: 78) cm
Sleeve seam 10 (12: 13: 15) in, 25 (31: 33: 38) cm

TENSION

18 sts and 28 rows to 10 cm square on 4½mm needles measured over double moss st. (or size needed to obtain given tension).

SPECIAL ABBREVIATIONS

TW 2 – (Twist 2), K into front of 2nd st. on left hand needle, K first st. and slip loops off tog.
C3B – (Cross 3 Back), slip next 3 sts onto a cable needle and hold at back of work. K next st., then K3 sts from cable needle.
C3F – (Cross 3 Front), slip next st. onto a cable needle and hold at front of work, K3 sts, then K st. from cable needle.
C6 – (Cable 6), slip next 3 sts onto a cable needle and hold at front of work, K3 sts, then K3 sts. from cable needle.
C3R – (Cross 3 right), slip next st. onto a cable needle and hold at back of work, K2 sts, then K st. from cable needle.
C3L – (Cross 3 left), slip next 2 sts onto a cable needle and hold at front of work, P1, then K2 sts from cable needle.

BACK

With 3¾mm needles cast on 67 (71: 75: 79) sts. Work 2 (2: 2½: 2½) in, 5 (5: 6.5: 6.5) cm, in K1 P1 rib. On the last row inc. 17 sts evenly. [84 (88: 92: 96) sts].
Change to 4½mm needles and commence patt. as follows. (The symbol † will be referred to on the sleeves and bag.)
1st row – K1, (P1, K1) 1 (2: 3: 4) times, P1, TW2, P1, K9, P1, TW2, † P1, TW2, P1, K6, P1, TW2, P8, K4, P8, TW2, P1, K6, P1, TW2, P1, † TW2, P1, K9, P1, TW2 (P1, K1) to end.
2nd row – P1, (K1, P1) 1 (2: 3: 4) times, K1, P2, K1, P9, K1, P2, † K1, P2, K1, P6, K1, P2, K8, P4, K8, P2, K1, P6, K1, P2, K1, † P2, K1, P9, K1, P2, (K1 P1) to end.
3rd row – P1, (K1, P1) 1 (2: 3: 4) times, P1, TW2, P1, C3B, K1, C3F, P1, TW2, † P1, TW2, P1, K6, P1, TW2, P7, C3R, C3L, P7, TW2, P1, K6, P1, TW2, P1, † TW2, P1, C3B, K1, C3F, P1, TW2, P2, (K1 P1) to end.
4th row – K1 (P1, K1) 1 (2: 3: 4) times, K1, P2, K1, P9, K1, P2, † K1, P2, K1, P6, K1, P2, K7, P2, (K1, P1) P2, K7, P2, K1, P6, K1, P2, K1 † P2, K1, P9, K1, P2, K2 (P1, K1)
5th row – K1, (P1, K1) 1 (2: 3: 4) times, P1, TW2, P1, K9, P1, TW2, † P1, TW2, P1, C6, P1, TW2, P6, C3R (P1, K1) C3L, P6, TW2, P1, C6, P1, TW2, P1 †, TW2, P1, K9, P1, TW2, (P1, K1) to end.
6th row – P1 (K1, P1) 1 (2: 3: 4) times, K1, P2, K1, P9, K1, P2, † K1, P2, K1, P6, K1, P2, K6, P2, (K1, P1) twice, P2, K6, P2, K1, P6, K1, P2, K1, † P2, K1, P9, K1, P2 (K1, P1) to end.
7th row – P1 (K1, P1) 1 (2: 3: 4) times, P1, TW2, P1, C3B, K1, C3F, P1, TW2, † P1, TW2, P1, K6, P1, TW2, P5, C3R (P1, K1) twice, C3L, P5, TW2, P1, K6, P1, TW2, P1, † TW2, P1, C3B, K1, C3F, P1, TW2, P2, (K1, P1) to end.
8th row – K1 (P1, K1) 1 (2: 3: 4) times, K1 P2, K1, P9, K1, P2 † K1, P2, K1, P6, K1, P2, K5, P2 (K1, P1) 3 times, P2, K5, P2, K1, P6, K1, P2, K1, † P2, K1, P9, K1, P2, K2, (P1, K1) to end.
9th row – K1 (P1, K1) 1 (2: 3: 4) times, P1, TW2, P1, K9, P1, TW2, † P1, TW2, P1, K6, P1, TW2, P4, C3R, (P1, K1) 3 times, C3L, P4, TW2, P1, K6, P1, TW2, P1, † TW2, P1, K9, P1, TW2, (P1, K1) to end.
10th row – P1 (K1 P1) 1 (2: 3: 4) times, K1, P2, K1, P9, K1, P2, † K1, P2, K1, P6, K1, P2, K4, P2 (K1, P1) 4 times, P2, K4, P2, K1, P6, K1, P2, K1, † P2, K1, P9, K1, P2, (K1, P1) to end.
11th row – P1 (K1, P1) 1 (2: 3: 4) times, P1, TW2, P1, C3B, K1, C3F, P1, TW2, † P1, TW2, P1, C6, P1, TW2, P3, C3R, (P1, K1) 4 times, C3L, P3, TW2, P1, C6, P1, TW2, P1, † TW2, P1, C3B, K1, C3F, P1, TW2, P2 (K1, P1) to end.
12th row – K1 (P1, K1) 1 (2: 3: 4) times, K1, P2, K1, P9, K1, P2, † K1, P2, K1, P6, K1, P2, K3, P2, (K1, P1) 5 times, P2, K3, P2, K1, P6, K1, P2, K1, † P2, K1, P9, K1, P2, K2 (P1 K1) to end.
13th row – K1 (P1, K1) 1 (2: 3: 4) times, P1, TW2, P1, K9, P1, TW2, † P1, TW2, P1, K6, P1, TW2, P2, C3R, (P1, K1) 5 times, C3L, P2, TW2, P1, K6, P1, TW2, P1, † TW2, P1, K9, P1, TW2, (P1, K1) to end.
14th row – P1 (K1, P1) 1 (2: 3: 4) times, K1, P2, K1, P9, K1, P2, † K1, P2, K1, P6, K1, P2, K2, P2, (K1, P1) 6 times, P2, K2, P2, K1, P6, K1, P2, K1, † P2, K1, P9, K1, P2, (K1, P1) to end.
15th row – P1 (K1 P1) 1 (2: 3: 4) times, P1, TW2, P1, C3B, K1, C3F, P1, TW2, † P1, TW2, P1, K6, P1, TW2, P2, C3L, (K1, P1) 5 times, C3R, P2, TW2, P1, K6, P1, TW2, P1, † TW2, P1, C3B, K1, C3F, P1, TW2, P2 (K1, P1) to end.
16th row – K1 (P1, K1) 1 (2: 3: 4) times, K1, P2, K1, P9, K1, P2, † K1, P2, K1, P6, K1, P2, K3, P2, (K1, P1) 5 times, P2, K3, P2, K1, P6, K1, P2, K1, † P2, K1, P9, K1, P2, K2, (P1, K1) to end.
17th row – K1 (P1, K1) 1 (2: 3: 4) times, P1, TW2, P1, K9, P1, TW2, † P1, TW2, P1, C6, P1, TW2, P3, C3L, (K1, P1) 4 times, C3R, P3, TW2, P1, C6, P1, TW2, P1, † TW2, P1, K9, P1, TW2, (P1, K1) to end.
18th row – P1 (K1, P1) 1 (2: 3: 4) times, K1, P2, K1, P9, K1, P2, † K1, P2, K1, P6, K1, P2, K4, P2 (K1, P1) 4 times, P2, K4, P2, K1, P6, K1, P2, K1, † P2, K1, P9, K1, P2 (K1, P1) to end.
19th row – P1 (K1, P1) 1 (2: 3: 4) times, P1, TW2, P1, C3B, K1, C3F, P1, TW2, † P1, TW2, P1, K6, P1, TW2, P4, C3L, (K1, P1) 3 times, C3R, P4, TW2, P1, K6, P1, TW2, P1, † TW2, P1, C3B, K1, C3F, P1, TW2, P2 (K1, P1) to end.
20th row – K1 (P1, K1) 1 (2: 3: 4) times, K1, P2, K1, P9, K1, P2, † K1, P2, K1,

P6, K1, P2, K5, P2, (K1, P1) 3 times, P2, K5, P2, K1, P6, K1, P2, K1, † P2, K1, P9, K1, P2, K2, (P1, K1) to end.
21st row – K1 (P1, K1) 1 (2: 3: 4) times, P1, TW2, P1, K9, P1, TW2, † P1, TW2, P1, K6, P1, TW2, P5, C3L (K1, P1) twice, C3R, P5, TW2, P1, K6, P1, TW2, P1, † TW2, P1, K9, P1, TW2 (P1, K1) to end.
22nd row – P1 (K1, P1) 1 (2: 3: 4) times, K1, P2, K1, P9, K1, P2, † K1, P2, K1, P6, K1, P2, K6, P2, (K1, P1) twice, P2, K6, P2, K1, P6, K1, P2, K1, † P2, K1, P9, K1, P2, (K1 P1) to end.
23rd row – P1 (K1, P1) 1 (2: 3: 4) times, P1, TW2, P1, C3B, K1, C3F, P1, TW2, † P1, TW2, P1, C6, P1, TW2, P6, C3L, (K1, P1), C3R, P6, TW2, P1, C6, P1, TW2, P1, † TW2, P1, C3B, K1, C3F, P1, TW2, P2, (K1, P1) to end.
24th row – K1 (P1, K1) 1 (2: 3: 4) times, K1, P2, K1, P9, K1, P2, † K1, P2, K1, P6, K1, P2, K7, P2, (K1, P1) P2, K7, P2, K1, P6, K1, P2, K1, † P2, K1, P9, K1, P2, K2 (P1, K1) to end.
25th row – K1 (P1, K1) 1 (2: 3: 4) times, P1, TW2, P1, K9, P1, TW2, † P1, TW2, P1, K6, P1, TW2, P7, C3L, C3R, P7, TW2, P1, K6, P1, TW2, P1, † TW2, P1, K9, P1, TW2 (P1, K1) to end.
Rows 2–25 (inclusive) form patt.
Keeping continuity of patt.
(throughout) rep. these rows until work measures 16½ (18: 20½: 23) in, 42 (46: 52: 58) cm. from beg. ending with a wrong side row.

⭕ To shape Raglans

Keeping patt. correct cast off 3 sts at beg. of next 2 rows.
3rd row – K1, K2tog, t.b.l. patt. to last 3 sts., K2tog, K1.
4th row – P1, P2tog, patt. to last 3 sts. P2tog tbl., P1.
Rep 3rd and 4th rows until 54 (58: 66: 78) sts remain.
Next row – K1, K2tog tbl, patt. to last 3 sts, K2tog, K1.
Next row – P2, patt. to last 2 sts, P2.
Rep. the last 2 rows until 30 (30: 32: 34) sts remain.
Next row – P2 (2: 3: 4)⋆, P2 tog, P4 ⋆ rep from ⋆ to ⋆ 4 more times, P2 tog, P2 (2: 3: 4).
Leave rem. 24 (24: 26: 28) sts on a holder.

FRONT

Work exactly as given for back until 44 (44: 48: 52) sts. rem. on raglan shaping, ending with a wrong side row.

⭕ To shape neck

Next row – K1, K2tog tbl, patt. 12 (12: 13: 14) sts, turn and work on these sts only.
⋆⋆ Cont. to dec. every alt. row at raglan edge as before, and at the same time

dec. 1 st. at the neck edge on every row until 5 (5: 6: 7) sts remain.
Dec. at raglan edge only as before until 2 sts remain. P2tog and fasten off.
With RS work facing sl. next 14 (14: 16: 18) sts onto a holder. Rejoin yarn to remaining sts.
Next row – patt. to last 3 sts, K2tog tbl, K1.
Complete to match first side from ⋆⋆ to end.

SLEEVES

With 3¾mm needles cast on 33 (33: 35: 35) sts. Work 2 (2: 2½: 2½) in, 5 (5: 6.5: 6.5) cm in K1 P1 rib. On the last row inc. 13 (13: 11: 11) sts evenly. [46 sts].
Change to 4½mm needles and commence patt. as follows.
1st row – Work from † to †, on 1st patt. row for back.
2nd row – Work from † to †, on 2nd patt. row for back.
Cont. working in patt. between symbols †, on patt. for back. At the same time inc. 1 st. at both ends of the 5th patt. row and then every foll. 6th row until 56 (60: 66: 62) sts, then every 10th row until 60 (64: 68: 68) sts, working extra sts. in double moss st.
Work without further shaping until sleeve measures 10 (12: 13: 15) in, 25 (31: 33: 38) cm, or required length from beg. ending with a wrong side row.

⭕ To shape top

Keeping patt. correct, cast off 3 sts at beg. of next 2 rows.
3rd row – K1, K2 tog tbl, patt. to last 3 sts, K2tog, K1.
4th row – P1, P2tog, patt. to last 3 sts, P2tog tbl, P1.
Rep. 3rd and 4th rows until 30 (34: 42: 50) sts remain.
Next row – K1, K2 tog tbl, patt. to last 3 sts, K2tog, K1.
Next row – P2, patt. to last 2 sts, P2.
Rep. the last 2 rows until 6 (6: 8: 6) sts remain, leave on a holder.

NECKBAND

Join raglan seams leaving left back seam open.
With 3¾mm needles and RS work facing pick up and K6 (6: 8: 6) sts from left sleeve top, 13 (13: 15: 17) sts down left front neck. Dec. 5 sts across centre front as follows.
K2 (2: 3: 4) sts, (K2tog) 5 times. K2 (2: 3: 4) sts. Pick up and K13 (13: 15: 17) sts up right front neck, 6 (6: 8: 6) sts from right sleeve top and 24 (24: 26: 28) sts from back neck.
[71 (71: 83: 87) sts]. Work 2 (2: 2½: 2½) in., 5 (5: 6.5: 6.5) cm, in K1 P1 rib. Cast off loosely in rib.

TO MAKE UP

Press work according to yarn instructions, omitting ribbing. Sew up left back raglan seam and neckband. Fold neckband in half and sew down on wrong side.
Sew up side and sleeve seams.

BAG

MATERIALS

Yarn 2 × 50g Pingouin Orage
Needles 1 pair 4½mm (UK 7)
1 cable needle.

MEASUREMENTS

9½in × 10 in (24 × 25 cm)

FRONT

Cast on 46 sts.
Work rows 1–25 between symbols † on patt. for back. Rep. rows 2–25 once more. Work 6 rows g. st. (every row K). Cast off.

BACK

Cast on 50 sts. Work in g. st. until length measures same as front. Cast off.

TO MAKE UP

Press work according to yarn instructions.
Sew up seams. Make strap using 4 strands yarn twisted together. Make two pompons and sew on sides of bag.

HAT

MATERIALS

Yarn 2 (3) × 50g Pingouin Orage
Needles 1 pair 3¼mm (UK 10)
1 pair 4mm (UK 8)
1 cable needle.

MEASUREMENTS

To fit head 18 (22) in, 46 (56) cm.

TENSION

20 sts and 28 rows to 10 cm square on 4mm needles measured over st. st. (or size needed to obtain given tension).

45

SPECIAL ABBREVIATIONS

TW2B – (Twist 2 back) slip next st. onto cable needle and hold at back of work, KB1, then P1 from cable needle.
TW2F – (Twist 2 front) slip next st. onto cable needle and hold at front of work, P1, then KB1 from cable needle.
KB1 – Knit into back of next st.
PB1 – Purl into back of next st.

INSTRUCTIONS

With 3¼mm needles cast on 81 (101) sts. Work 5in (13 cm) in K1 P1 rib. On the last row inc. 9 (11) sts evenly [90 (112) sts].
Change to 4mm needles and commence patt. as follows.
1st row – K1, * P3, TW2B, K1, TW2F, P3, ** rep. from * to last st., K1.
2nd row – K1, * K3, PB1, K1, P1, K1, PB1, K3, ** rep from * to last st., K1.
3rd row – K1, * P2, TW2B, K1, P1, K1, TW2F, P2, ** rep. from * to last st., K1.
4th row – K1, * K2, PB1, (K1 P1) twice, K1, PB1, K2 ** rep. from * to last st., K1.
5th row – K1, * P1, TW2B, (K1, P1) twice, K1, TW2F, P1, ** rep. from * to last st., K1.
6th row – K1, * K1, PB1, (K1, P1) 3 times, K1, PB1, K1, ** rep. from * to last st., K1.
7th row – K1, * TW2B, (K1, P1) 3 times, K1, TW2F, ** rep. from * to last st., K1.
8th row – K1, * PB1, (K1, P1) 4 times, K1, PB1, ** rep. from * to last st., K1.
9th row – K1, * TW2F, (P1, K1) 3 times, P1, TW2B, ** rep. from * to last st., K1.
10th row – As 6th row.
11th row – K1, * P1, TW2F, (P1, K1) twice, P1, TW2B, P1, ** rep. from * to last st., K1.
12th row – As 4th row.
13th row – K1, * P2, TW2F, P1, K1, P1, TW2B, P2, ** rep. from * to last st., K1.
14th row – As 2nd row.
15th row – K1, * P3, TW2F, P1, TW2B, P3, ** rep. from * to last st., K1.
16th row – K1, * K4, PB1, K1, PB1, K4 ** rep. from * to last st., K1.
These 16 rows forms the patt.
Next row – K1, * P4, KB1, P1, KB1, P4, rep. from * to last st., K1.
Next row – K1, * K4, PB1, K1, PB1, K4, rep. from * to last st., K1.
Rep. the last 2 rows 1 (5) times more.
Keeping rib. correct between shapings, dec. thus;
1st row – K1, (P2, P2tog, KB1, P1, KB1, P2tog, P2) to last st., K1.
Work 3 rows.
5th row – K1, (P1, P2tog, KB1, P1, KB1, P2tog, P1) to last st., K1.
Work 3 rows.
9th row – K1, (P2tog, KB1, P1, KB1, P2tog) to last st., K1. [42 (52) sts].
Work 3 rows.
13th row – K2tog, (KB1, P1, KB1, P2tog) to end. [33 (41) sts].
Work 1 row.
15th row – K1, (K2tog) to end.
Purl 1 row. Break wool, thread through rem. sts. and draw up firmly.

TO MAKE UP

Press work according to yarn instructions, omitting ribbing.
Sew up seam. Make a pompon and sew to top of hat.

COLOURFUL CLASSICS

... next, a vivid green Aran sweater ...

MATERIALS

Yarn 8 (9, 10) × 50g balls Pingouin Pingostar
Needles 1 pair 3¾mm (UK 9)
1 pair 4½mm (UK 7)
1 cable needle.

MEASUREMENTS

To fit chest 27½ (30: 32½) in, 70 (76: 82) cm
Length 19 (21: 23¾) in, 48 (53: 60) cm
Sleeve seam 14¼ (15¼: 16½) in, 36 (39: 42) cm.

TENSION

20 sts and 20 rows to 10 cm square on 4½mm needles measured over pattern. (or size needed to obtain given tension).

SPECIAL ABBREVIATIONS

KB1, = Knit into back of next st.
PB1 = Purl into back of next st.
C2F = (Cross 2 front), with right needle, K 2nd stitch, on left needle then K first st., slipping both sts off needle tog.
C2B = (Cross 2 back), with right needle K 2nd stitch tbl, on left needle, then K first st. in usual way, slipping both sts. off needle tog.
C6F = (Cable 6 front), slip next 3 sts. onto a cable needle and hold at front of work. K next 3 sts, then K 3 sts. from cable needle.
C6B = (Cable 6 back), slip next 3 sts. onto a cable needle and hold at back of work. K. next 3 sts, then K3 sts. from cable needle.

BACK

With 3¾mm needles cast on 62 (70: 78) sts. Work 2¾ in. (7 cm) KB1, PB1 rib. On the last row inc. 20 sts. evenly [82 (90: 98) sts].
Next row – (wrong side). Change to 4½mm needles, then P5 (9: 13) sts, K2, P2, K2, P9, K2, P2, K2, P30, K2, P2, K2, P9, K2, P2, K2, P. rem. 5 (9: 13) sts.

Proceed in patt. as follows:
1st row – S1, (C2F, C2B) 1 (2: 3) times, P2, C2F, P2, C6F, K3, P2, C2B, P2, C6F (5 times), P2, C2F, P2, C6F, K3, P2, C2B, P2, C2F, C2B 1 (2: 3) times, K1.
2nd row – S1, P4 (8: 12) sts, K2, P2, K2, P9, K2, P2, K2, P30, K2, P2, K2, P9, K2, P2, K2, P4 (8: 12) sts, K1.
3rd row – S1, (C2B, C2F) 1 (2: 3) times, P2, C2F, P2, K9, P2, C2B, P2, K30, P2, C2F, P2, K9, P2, C2B, P2, (C2B, C2F) 1 (2: 3) times, K1.
4th row – As 2nd row.
5th row – S1, (C2F, C2B) 1 (2: 3) times, P2, C2F, P2, K3, C6B, P2, C2B, P2, K3, C6B (4 times), K3, P2, C2F, P2, K3, C6B, P2, C2B, P2, (C2F, C2B) 1 (2: 3) times, K1.
6th row – As 2nd row.
7th row – As 3rd row.
8th row – As 2nd row.
Rows 1–8 (inclusive) form patt.
Keeping continuity of patt. (throughout) cont. until work measures 11¾ (13: 14¼) in, 30 (33: 36) cm, from beg. ending on a right side row.

○ To shape armholes
On wrong side, rows dec. 1 st. at both ends, 1 stitch in from the edge, 3 (4: 5) times [76 (82: 88) sts].
Work straight until work measures 18 (20: 22) ins, 46 (51: 56) cm, from beg. ending on right side row.

○ To shape neck and shoulders
Next row – S1, patt 26 (29: 31) sts, cast off next 22 (22: 24) sts, patt. to last st. K1.
Work on last set of sts. as foll.
Next row – S1, patt. to last st., K1.
Next row – Cast off 6 sts. at neck edge, patt. to end.
Next row – S1, patt. to last st., K1.
Next row – Cast off rem. 21 (24: 26) sts for shoulder.
Rejoin yarn to rem. sts at neck edge and complete other side to match, reversing shaping.

FRONT

Work as given for back until work measures 16 (18: 20) in, 41 (46: 51) cm. from beg. ending on right side row.

○ To shape neck and shoulders

Next row – S1, patt. 29 (32: 34) sts. cast off next 16 (16: 18) sts, patt. to last st. K1.
Work on last set of sts. as foll.
Work 1 row.
Cast off at neck edge on next and foll. alt. rows, 3 sts twice, 2 sts once and 1 st. once.
Cont. straight until work measures 19 (21: 22¾) in, 48 (53: 58) cm. from beg. Cast off rem. 21 (24: 26) sts. for shoulder.
Rejoin yarn at neck edge and complete other side to match reversing shaping.

SLEEVES

With 3¾mm needles cast on 30 (32: 34) sts. Work 2¼ in. (6 cm) KB1, PB1 rib. On the last row inc. 16 sts. evenly [46 (48: 50) sts]
Next row – (wrong side). Change to 4½mm needles, then P2 (3: 4) sts, K2, P2, K2, P30, K2, P2, K2, P2 (3: 4) sts.
Proceed in patt. as foll.
1st row – K0 (1: 2), C2F, P2, C2B, P2, C6F (5 times), P2, C2F, P2, C2F, K0 (1:2).
2nd row – P 2 (3: 4), K2, P2, K2, P30, K2, P2, K2, P2 (3: 4).
3rd row – K0 (1: 2), C2B, P2, C2B, P2, K30, P2, C2F, P2, C2B, K0 (1: 2).
4th row – Inc. once in first st., P1 (2: 3), K2, P2, K2, P30, K2, P2, K2, P0 (1: 2), inc. once in next st., P1.
5th row – K1 (2: 3), C2F, P2, C2B, P2, K3, C6B (4 times), K3, P2, C2F, P2, C2F, K1 (2: 3).
6th row – P3 (4: 5), K2, P2, K2, P30, K2, P2, K2, P3 (4: 5)
7th row – K1 (2: 3), C2B, P2, C2B, P2, K30, P2, C2F, P2, C2B, K1 (2: 3).
8th row – As 6th row.
Rows 1–8 (inclusive) form patt.
Keeping continuity of patt. as set (throughout) inc. 1 st. at both ends on the next, then every foll. 5th row until 68 (74: 80) sts, working extra sts into C2F/C2B patt. Cont. straight until work measures 14¼ (15¼: 16½) in, 36 (39: 42) cm. from beg. ending on a right side row.

○ To shape top
On wrong side rows dec. 1 st. at both ends, 1 stitch in from the edge, 3 (4: 5) times. Cast off rem. 62 (66: 70) sts.

NECKBAND

Join left shoulder seam. With RS work facing and 3¾mm needles pick up and K48 (48: 50) sts along front neck edge and 36 (36: 38) sts along back neck. [84 (84: 88) sts]. Work 1¼in, (3 cm), in KB1, PB1 rib. Cast off loosely in rib.

MAKING UP

Press work according to yarn instructions omitting ribbing. Join right shoulder and neckband. Set in sleeves. Join side and sleeve seams.

COLOURFUL CLASSICS

... and the third Aran pattern, a practical zip-fronted cardigan.

MATERIALS

Yarn 8 (9: 10: 11) × 50g balls Double Knitting main colour
Small amounts in contrasts A, B, C.
Needles 1 pair 3mm (UK 11)
1 pair 4½mm (UK 7)
1 cable needle
1 open-ended zip to fit front of cardigan.

MEASUREMENTS

To fit chest 24 (26: 28: 30) in, 61 (66: 71: 76) cm.
Length 16 (17½: 18½: 20) in, 41 (44: 47: 50) cm.
Sleeve seam 10½ (12½: 14: 16) in, 27 (32: 36: 41) cm.

TENSION

20 sts and 28 rows to 10 cm square on 4½mm needles measured over double moss stitch (or size needed to obtain given tension).

SPECIAL ABBREVIATIONS

KB1 = Knit into back of next st.
PB1 = Purl into back of next st.
T3F = (Twist 3 front), slip next 2 sts. onto a cable needle and hold at front of work. P next st., then K2 sts from cable needle.
T3B = (Twist 3 back), slip next st. onto a cable needle and hold at back of work. K. next 2 sts, then P st. from cable needle.
T5F = (Twist 5 front), slip next 2 sts onto a cable needle and hold at front of work, P1, K2 from left needle, then K2 sts, from cable needle.
C4F = (Cable 4 front), slip next 2 sts. onto a cable needle and hold at front of work, K. next 2 sts, then K 2 sts from cable needle.

STRIPE PATTERN 1

(in rib)
4 rows MC, 4 rows A, 2 rows B, 2 rows C, 2 rows B, 4 rows A, 4 rows MC.

STRIPE PATTERN 2

(in rib – neckband).
2 rows MC, 2 rows A, 2 rows B, 2 rows C, 2 rows B, 2 rows A, 2 rows MC.

DIAMOND PANEL PATTERN

(worked over 21 sts)
1st row – K4, P4, T3B, K2, P4, K4.
2nd row – P4, K4, P2, K1, P2, K4, P4.
3rd row – C4F, P3, T3B, K1, T3F, P3, C4F.
4th row – P4, K3, P2, K1, P1, K1, P2, K3, P4.
5th row – K4, P2, T3B, K1, P1, K1, T3F, P2, K4.
6th row – P4, K2, P2, (K1, P1) twice, K1, P2, K2, P4.
7th row – C4F, P1, T3B, (K1, P1) twice, K1, T3F, P1, C4F.
8th row – P4, K1, P2 (K1, P1) 3 times, K1, P2, K1, P4.
9th row – K4, P1, T3F (P1, K1) twice, P1, T3B, P1, K4.
10th row – As 6th row.
11th row – C4F, P2, T3F, P1, K1, P1, T3B, P2, C4F.
12th row – As 4th row.
13th row – K4, P3, T3F, P1, T3B, P3, K4.
14th row – As 2nd row.
15th row – C4F, P4, T5F, P4, C4F.
16th row – P4, K4, P4, K5, P4.
These 16 rows form panel patt.

BACK

With 3mm needles and MC cast on 80 (86: 88: 94) sts. Work rows of *stripe patt* 1 in KB1, PB1, rib. On the last row inc. 15 (13: 19: 17) sts evenly. [95 (99: 107: 111) sts].
Change to 4½mm needles and commence patt. as follows.
1st row – (RS), (K1, P1) 2 (3: 5: 6) times, ★ work 1st row of diamond panel patt., P1, rep. from ★ twice more, work 1st row of diamond panel, (P1, K1) 2 (3: 5: 6) times.
2nd row – (P1, K1) 2 (3: 5: 6) times, ★ work 2nd row diamond panel, K1, rep. from ★ twice more, work 2nd row diamond panel, (K1, P1) 2 (3: 5: 6) times.
3rd row – (P1, K1) 1 (2: 4: 5) times, P2, ★ work 3rd row diamond panel, P1, rep from ★ twice more, work 3rd row diamond panel, P2, (K1, P1) 1 (2: 4: 5) times.
4th row – (K1, P1) 1 (2: 4: 5) times, K2, ★ work 4th row diamond panel, K1, rep from ★ twice more, work 4th row diamond panel, K2, (P1, K1) 1 (2: 4: 5) times.
The last 4 rows form the patt. for the double moss st. at each end of rows.
Rep. these 4 rows, at the same time cont. the diamond panels as set. until back measures 11 (12: 12½: 13½) in, 28 (30: 32: 34) cm from beg. ending with a WS row.

◯ To shape armholes

Cast off 2 (2: 3: 3) sts at beg. next 2 rows and 2 sts at beg. foll. 2 rows. Dec. 1 st. at both ends of next 7 rows, then every alt. row until 71 (75: 79: 83) sts. rem. Work straight until armhole measures 5 (5½: 6: 6½) ins, 13 (14: 15: 16) cm, ending with a WS row.

◯ To shape shoulders

Cast off 8 (8: 8: 9) sts. patt. 16 (17: 18: 18) sts (including st. already on needle), turn and complete this side first.
★ *Next row* – P2tog, patt. to end.
Next row – Cast off 8 (8: 8: 9) sts, patt. to last 2 sts, K2tog. Work 1 row. Cast off rem. 6 (7: 8: 7) sts.
Slip centre 23 (25: 27: 29) sts. onto a holder for neckband. With RS facing rejoin yarn to next st. and patt. to end.
Next row – Cast off 8 (8: 8: 9) sts, patt. to end.
Complete to match first side from ★ to end.

LEFT FRONT

★★ With 3mm needles and MC cast on 41 (45: 45: 49) sts. Work rows of *stripe patt.* 1 in KB1, PB1 rib. On the last row inc. 8 (6: 10: 8) evenly [49 (51: 55: 57) sts].★★
Change to 4½mm needles and commence patt. as foll.
1st row – (K1, P1) 2 (3: 5: 6) times, ★ work 1 st. row of diamond panel patt, across next 21 sts, ★ P1, rep. from ★ to ★ K2.
2nd row – K2, ★ work 2nd row of diamond panel patt. ★ K1, rep. from ★ to ★, (K1, P1) 2 (3: 5: 6) times.
3rd row – (P1, K1) 1 (2: 4: 5) times, P2, ★ work 3rd row of diamond panel patt, ★ P1, rep from ★ to ★, K2.

49

4th row – K2, * work 4th row of diamond panel patt.* K1, rep. from * to *, K2, (P1, K1) 1 (2: 4: 5) times.
Rep. these 4 rows, at the same time cont. diamond panels as set; until front measures same as back to armhole ending with a WS row.

○ To shape armholes

Cast off 2 (2: 3: 3) sts. at beg. next row and 2 sts at beg. foll. alt. row. Work 1 row. Dec. 1 st. at armhole edge on next 7 rows, then every alt. row until 37 (39: 41: 43) sts remain. Work straight until armhole measures 3½ (4: 4: 4½) ins, 9 (10: 10: 11) cm. ending at front edge.

○ To shape neck

Patt. 9 (10: 9: 10) sts, leave these sts on a holder for neckband, patt to end of row.
Dec. 1 st. at neck edge on next 5 rows, then every alt. row until 22 (23: 24: 25) sts remain. Work straight until front measures same as back to shoulder ending at armhole edge.

○ To shape shoulder

Cast off 8 (8: 8: 9) sts. at beg. of next and foll. alt. row.
Work 1 row. Cast off rem. 6 (7: 8: 7) sts.

RIGHT FRONT

Work as for Left front from ** to **.
Change to 4½mm needles and commence patt. as follows.
1st row – K2, * work 1st row of diamond panel patt. across next 21 sts, * P1, rep. from * to *, (P1, K1) 2 (3: 5: 6) times.
2nd row – (P1, K1) 2 (3: 5: 6) times, * work 2nd row of diamond panel patt, * K1, rep from * to *, K2.
3rd row – K2, * work 3rd row of diamond panel patt, * P1, rep from * to *, P2, (K1 P1) 1 (2: 4: 5) times.
4th row – (K1, P1) 1 (2: 4: 5) times, K2, * work 4th row of diamond panel patt, * K1, rep. from * to *, K2.
Rep. these 4 rows and cont. diamond panels as set. Complete to match left front reversing all shapings.

SLEEVES

With 3mm needles and MC cast on 47 (49: 49: 53) sts. Work rows of *stripe patt* 1. in KB1, PB1 rib. On the last row inc. 10 (12: 12: 12) sts. evenly. [57 (61: 61: 65) sts].
Change to 4½mm needles and commence patt. as foll.
1st row – (K1 P1) 9 (10: 10: 11) times, work 1st row of diamond panel patt. across next 21 sts, (P1, K1) 9 (10: 10: 11) times.
2nd row – (P1, K1) 9 (10: 10: 11) times, work 2nd row of diamond panel patt. (K1, P1) 9 (10: 10: 11) times.

3rd row – (P1, K1) 8 (9: 9: 10) times, P2, work 3rd row of diamond panel patt., P2, (K1, P1) 8 (9: 9: 10) times.
4th row – (K1, P1) 8 (9: 9: 10) times, K2, work 4th row of diamond panel patt, K2, (P1, K1) 8 (9: 9: 10) times.
Rep. these 4 rows, at the same time cont. the diamond panel as set until sleeve measures 10½ (12½: 14: 16) ins, 27 (32: 36: 41) cms from beg., ending with a WS row.

○ To shape top

Cast off 2 (2: 3: 3) sts at beg. next 2 rows. Dec. 1 st. at both ends of next 7 (7: 5: 5) rows, then every alt. row until 33 sts. rem.
Work 1 row. Dec. 1 st. at both ends of next 5 rows.
Cast off 3 sts. at beg. next 2 rows. Cast off rem. sts.

NECKBAND

Join shoulder seams. With 3mm needles, MC and RS work facing slip 9 (10: 9: 10) sts from holder at right front neck onto needle, rejoin yarn and pick up and K16 (16: 20: 20) sts. up right front neck, 4 sts down right back neck, 23 (25: 27: 29) sts across back neck, 4 sts down left back, 16 (16: 20: 20) sts down left front neck and 9 (10: 9: 10) sts from holder at left front neck. [81 (85: 93: 97) sts].
Work rows of *stripe patt* 2 in K1B, P1B, rib.
Cast off loosely in rib.

TO MAKE UP

Press work according to yarn instructions on the wrong side, omitting ribbing. Join side and sleeve seams. Set in sleeves. Insert zip.

RAINBOW FAIR ISLE

All the colours of the rainbow make a splendid pattern on this Fair Isle slipover, our fourth 'colourful classic'.

MATERIALS

Yarn 3 (3: 4) × 50g 4 ply main colour (pale grey)
1 (1: 2) × 50g contrast A (black)
1 × 50g ball of each, contrast B – lilac, C – royal blue, D – green, E – yellow, F – orange, G – red, H – purple.
Needles 1 pair 2¾mm (UK 12)
1 pair 3¼mm (UK 10)
Set of 4 needles size 2¾mm (UK 12)

MEASUREMENTS

To fit chest 26 (28: 30) in, 66(71: 76) cm
Length 17 (18¼: 19¼) in, 43 (46: 49) cm

TENSION

28 sts and 36 rows to 10 cm square on 3¼mm needles (or size needed to obtain given tension).

BACK

With 2¾mm needles and MC cast on 96 (104: 112) sts.
Work 2 in (5 cm) in K2 P2 rib. **
Change to 3¼mm needles and starting with a K row, work *Stripe Patt.* in st. st. as follows:
Work * 2 rows con A, 14 rows MC. * rep from * to *. throughout.
Keeping continuity of stripe patt. (throughout) cont. straight until work measures 11½ (12¼: 13) in, 29 (31: 33) cm from beg. ending with a P row.

○ To shape armholes
Cast off 7 sts. at beg. of next 2 rows., Dec. 1 st. at both ends of next and foll. 6 alt. rows [68 (76: 84) sts].
Keeping stripe patt. correct work straight until armhole measures 5½ (6: 6¼) in, 14 (15: 16) cm, ending with a P row.

○ To shape shoulders
Cast off 5 (6: 7) sts at beg of next 4 rows, and 5 (5: 6) sts. at beg. of next 2 rows.
Leave rem. 38 (42: 44) sts. on a holder.

FRONT

Work as given for back to **. Change to 3¼mm needles, and starting with a K row, work in st. st.
Joining in contrasts where necessary work rows of rainbow patt. from chart across all sts. Rows 1–18 (inclusive) form patt. Rep. rows 3–18 (inclusive) throughout.
Keeping continuity of patt. (throughout) cont. straight until work measures 11½ (12¼: 13) in. 29 (31: 33) cm from beg. ending with a P row.

○ To shape armholes
Cast off 7 sts. at beg. of next 2 rows.
Dec. 1 st. at both ends of next and foll. 2 alt. rows. 76 (84: 92) sts.
Work 1 row.

○ To divide for neck
Next row – Sl. 1, K1, psso, patt. 36 (40: 44) sts, turn, and complete this side first.
*** Dec. 1 st. at neck edge on next and every foll. alt. row. At the same time dec. 1 st. at armhole edge on alt. rows as before, 3 more times.
Keeping armhole edge straight, cont. neck dec. as before until 15 (17: 20) sts rem.
Work straight until length measures same as back to shoulder, ending at armhole edge.

○ To shape shoulder
Cast off 5 (6: 7) sts. at beg. of next and foll. alt. row.
Work 1 row. Cast off 5 (5: 6) sts.
With RS work facing rejoin yarn to rem. sts. and patt. to last 2 sts, K2tog.
Complete to match first side from *** to end.

NECKBAND

Sew up shoulder seams.
With RS work facing, set of 4 2¾mm needles and MC, pick up and K50 (54: 56) sts up right side of neck, 38 (42: 44) sts from back neck and 50 (54: 56) sts down left side neck. [138 (150: 156) sts].
Working rows back and forth, work 2 in (5 cm) in K2 P2 rib. Cast off loosely in rib.

ARMBANDS

With RS work facing, 2¾mm needles and MC, pick up and K102 (110: 116) sts evenly along armhole edges. Work 2 in (5 cm) in K2 P2 rib. Cast off loosely in rib.

TO MAKE UP

Press work according to yarn instructions omitting ribbing.
Fold neckband in half and sew down on wrong side, crossing neckband over at front as shown.
Sew up side seams and armbands. Fold armbands in half and sew down on wrong side.

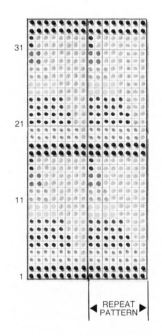

LITTLE GOLFER

A modern version of a traditional Argyll pattern is our fifth Scottish classic.

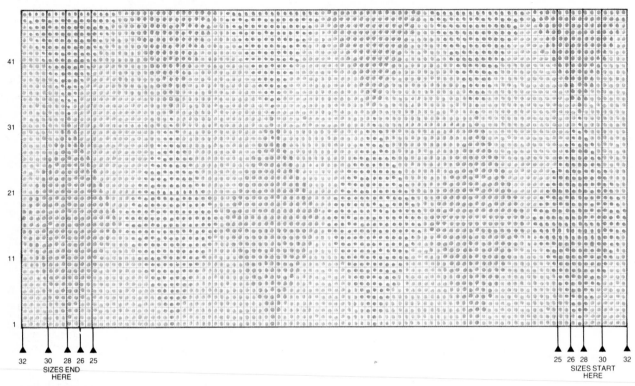

41
31
21
11
1

32   30   28 26 25
SIZES END
HERE

25 26 28   30   32
SIZES START
HERE

MATERIALS

Yarn 4 (4: 5: 5: 6) × 50g Main Colour
Pingouin Pingostar – grey
2 × 50g Contrast A – blue
2 × 50g Contrast B – pink.
Small amount colour – (red) for stitching.
Needles 1 pair 3¾mm (UK 9)
1 pair 4½mm (UK 7)

MEASUREMENTS

To fit chest 25 (26: 28: 30: 32) in, 63
(66: 71: 76: 81) cm.
Length 15 (16: 17½: 18½: 20½) in, 38
(41: 44: 47: 52) cm.
Sleeve seam 10 (11½: 13: 14: 15½) in,
25 (29: 33: 36: 40) cm.

TENSION

19 sts and 25 rows to 10 cm square on
4½mm needles (or size needed to
obtain given tension).

BACK

With 3¾mm needles and Con A cast on
64 (68: 72: 78: 86) sts.

Working in K1, P1 rib, work 2 rows A
then 10 rows in MC.
On the last row inc. 9 sts evenly. [73
(77: 81: 87: 95) sts]. ★
Change to 4½mm needles, cont. in MC
and starting with a K row, work in st.
st. Cont. straight until work measures 9
(9½: 10½: 11½: 12½) in, 23 (24: 27:
29: 32) cm. from beg. ending with a P
row. Place col. marker at each end of
last row to position armholes.
Cont. straight until work measures 14½
(15¾: 17: 18: 20) in. 37 (40: 43: 46:
51) cm from beg. ending with a P row.

○ To shape neck
Next row – K31 (33: 35: 38: 42) sts. Cast
off 11 sts. K to end.
Work on last set of sts. as follows:
Next row – Purl.
Next row – Cast off 8 (8: 8: 9: 10) sts.
at neck edge, K to end.
Next row – Purl.
Cast off rem. 23 (25: 27: 29: 32) sts. for
shoulder.
Rejoin yarn at neck edge and complete
other side to match reversing shaping.

FRONT

Work as given for back to ★.
Change to 4½mm needles and purl one
row.
Starting with a K row, work in st. st.
and commence patt. as follows:
Work rows 1–32 (inclusive) from chart
as indicated, twisting yarns together
when changing col.
These 32 rows form the patt. Repeating
them and keeping continuity of patt.
(throughout) cont. until work measures
same as back to markers, for armhole
positions.
Place col. markers as before. Cont.
straight until work measures 12¼
(13½: 14½: 15½: 17) in., 31 (34: 37:
39: 43) cm from beg. ending with a P
row.

○ To shape neck
Patt. 31 (33: 35: 38: 42) sts. Cast off 11
sts. patt. to end.
Work on last set of sts. as follows:
Work 1 row.
Cast off at neck edge on next and foll.
alt rows, 3 sts 1 (1: 2: 2: 3) times, 2 sts
2 (2: 1: 1: 0) times and 1 st. 1 (1: 1: 2:
2) times. [23 (25: 26: 28: 31) sts].
Cont. straight until length measures
same as back to shoulder, ending with
a P row. Cast off.
Rejoin yarn at neck edge to rem. sts.
and complete to match first side
reversing all shapings.

SLEEVES

With 3¾mm needles and Con. A cast
on 36 (36: 36: 40: 42) sts.
Working in K1 P1 rib, work 2 rows A,
then 8 rows MC. On the last row inc.
12 sts evenly [48 (48: 48: 52: 54) sts].
Change to 4½mm needles and starting
with a K row work in st. st. Inc. 1 st.
at both ends of next and every foll. 6th
(8th: 6th: 8th: 6th) rows until 60 (64:
68: 72: 80) sts.

Cont. straight until work measures 10
(11½: 13: 14: 15½) in, 25 (29: 33: 36:
40) cm from beg. ending with a P row.
Cast off.

NECKBAND

Join left shoulder seam. With RS work
facing, 3¾mm needles and MC pick
up and K74 (74: 78: 86: 90) sts evenly
around neck. Working in K1 P1 rib,
work 6 rows MC., then 1 row Con A.

Cast off in Con A.

TO MAKE UP

Press work according to yarn
instructions, omitting ribbing.
Sew up right shoulder and neckband.
Sew in sleeves between markers.
Sew up side and sleeve seams.
Work contrast stitching on front as
shown in photograph.

55

LITTLE MENACE

Diabolical stripes give an authentic look to this Dennis the Menace sweater, hat and leg-warmers.

SWEATER

MATERIALS

Yarn 4 (5: 5: 6) × 50g Pingouin Pingofrance (red) A
4 (5: 5: 6) × 50g (black) B
Needles 1 pair 3mm (UK 11)
1 pair 3¾mm (UK 9)

MEASUREMENTS

To fit bust/chest 30 (32: 34: 36) in, 76 (81: 87: 92) cm
Length 17¼ (18½: 19¾: 21) in, 44 (47: 50: 53) cm
Sleeve seam 13 (13¾: 14½: 15¼) in, 33 (35: 37: 39) cm

TENSION

23 sts and 42 rows to 10 cm square on 3¾mm needles (or size needed to obtain given tension) as measured over Fisherman rib.

PATTERN STITCHES

Fisherman rib – worked over an odd number of sts. as follows:
1st row – (RS) K all sts.
2nd row – K1, * P1, then K next st. in row below, inserting needle through work and allowing st. above to drop off needle; rep. from * to last 2 sts, P1, K1.
These 2 rows form patt.

Stripe pattern – used throughout sweater.
Alternating black and red stripes, each 34 rows wide.

BACK

With 3mm needles and A cast on 103 (109: 115: 121) sts. Work 2½in (6cm) in K1 P1 rib.
Change to 3¾mm needle and starting with B work rows of *Stripe patt.* in Fisherman rib. Cont. straight until work measures 10¼ (11: 11¾: 12½) in, 26 (28: 30: 32) cm, from beg. ending with a wrong side row.

○ To shape raglans
** Mark each end of last row with a coloured thread to indicate beg. of armhole.
Keeping stripe patt. correct shape raglans as follows:
1st – 4th rows – Work without shaping.
5th row – K3, K3tog, K to last 6 sts, sl. 1, K2tog, psso. K3.
6th row – As 2nd patt. row.
Rep. last 6 rows 3 times more.
25 – 26th rows – Work without shaping.
27th row – As 5th row.
28th row – As 2nd patt. row.
Rep. last 4 rows 12 (13: 14: 15) times **
Leave rem. 35 (37: 39: 41) sts. on a holder.

FRONT

Work as given for back until 47 (49: 51: 53) sts. rem. in raglan shaping.

○ To shape neck
Next row – K 16 sts, turn, leave rem. sts on a spare needle.
*** Dec. 1 st. at neck edge on next 3 rows and then next 3 alt. rows. At the same time, work raglan dec. as usual on 3rd and 7th rows of neck shaping [6 sts]. Work raglan dec. on next row.
Dec. 1 st. at neck edge on foll. row.
Cast off rem. 3 sts.
With RS facing sl. next 15 (17: 19: 21) sts. onto a spare needle. Rejoin yarn to next st. and K to end of row.
Complete to match first side from *** to end.

SLEEVES

With 3mm needles and B cast on 49 (49: 53: 53) sts. Work 2½ in. (6 cm) in K1 P1 rib.
Change to 3¾mm needles and starting with A work rows of *stripe patt.* in Fisherman rib. At the same time inc. 1 st. at both ends of every foll. 8th row 10 (8: 11: 9) times, then every foll. 6th row 4 (8: 5: 9) times, working extra sts. into patt. [77 (81: 85: 89) sts]. Cont. without further shaping until sleeve measures 13 (13¾: 14½: 15½) in., 33 (35: 37: 39) cm. from beg. ending with a wrong side row.

○ To shape raglan
Work as given for back from ** to **.
Leave rem. 9 sts on a holder.

ROLL NECKBAND

Join front raglan seams and right back seam. With RS work facing, 3 mm needles and A, pick up and K9 sts across left sleeve top, 15 sts down left front neck, 15 (17: 19: 21) sts from centre front, 15 sts up right front neck, 9 sts across right sleeve top and 35 (37: 39: 41) sts. from back neck. [98 (101: 106: 111) sts]. Work 3 in (7.5 cm) in g. st. (every row K). Cast off.

TO MAKE UP

Join left back raglan and neckband. Roll neckband to outside of neck. Join side and sleeve seams.

HAT

MATERIALS

Yarn 3 × 50g Pingouin Pingofrance (red) A
Small amount (black) B
Needles 1 pair 4mm (UK 8)

MEASUREMENTS

1 size to fit all.

TENSION

31 sts and 32 rows to 10 cm square on 4mm needles (or size needed to obtain given tension) as measured over K1 P1 rib.

INSTRUCTIONS

With A cast on 132 sts and work 10¼ in (26 cm) in K1 P1 rib.
Break off A and join in B.
Next row – Dec. row. * Rib 9 sts, rib 3 sts tog. rep from * to end of row.
Make a dec. above each of these dec. in the 6th row, 10th row, 12th row and 14th row. Run a strand of yarn through rem. sts. and draw up tightly.

TO MAKE UP

Sew up seam.

LEG-WARMERS

MATERIALS

Yarn 2 × 50g Pingouin Pingofrance
(red) A
1 × 50g (black) B
Needles 1 pair 3¼mm (UK 10)

MEASUREMENTS

Length 15 in (38 cm)

TENSION

20 sts and 28 rows to 10 cm square on
3¼mm needles (or size needed to
obtain given tension) as measured over
st. st.

INSTRUCTIONS

With A cast on 60 sts and work 4 in (10
cm) in K1 P1 rib.
Break off A, join in B and starting with
a K row, work in st. st. for 3 in (7.5
cm). Rejoin A and work another 3 in.
(7.5 cm).
Rejoin B and work a third stripe as
before. Break off B.
Rejoin A and work 2 in (5 cm) in K1
P1 rib. Cast off in rib.

TO MAKE UP

Sew up leg seams.

ON THE ROAD

For its wearer this jumper will be a real transport of delight.

SWEATER

MATERIALS

Yarn 6 (6: 7: 7: 8) × 50g 4 ply main
colour (yellow)
2 × 50g contrast A – black. Small
amounts contrasts B – grey, C – royal
blue, D – red, E – white, F – navy blue,
G – wine.
Needles 1 pair 2¾mm (UK 12)
1 pair 3¼mm (UK 10)

MEASUREMENTS

To fit bust/chest 30 (32: 34: 36: 38) in.,
76 (82: 87: 92: 97) cm
Length 20½ (21½: 22½: 23½: 25½)
in, 52 (55: 57: 60: 65) cm
Sleeve seam 16 (17: 18: 19: 19) in, 41
(43: 46: 48: 48) cm.

TENSION

28 sts and 36 rows to 10 cm square on
3¼mm needles (or size needed to
obtain given tension).

BACK

With 2¾mm needles and MC cast on
114 (120: 126: 132: 140) sts.
**Working in K2 P2 rib work 2 rows
MC, 3 rows con A, then 1¾ in (4 cm)
in MC. **
Change to 3¼mm needles and starting
with a K row, work in st. st. Cont.
straight until work measures 13½
(14½: 15½: 16½: 18) in. 34 (37: 39:
42: 46) cm. from beg. ending with a P
row.

○ To shape armholes
Inc. 1 st. at both ends of next and every
foll. 10th row, 6 times, [128 (134: 140:
146: 154) sts]. Work 5 (5: 5: 5: 7) rows
straight.

○ To shape shoulders
Cast off 6 (6: 7: 7: 6) sts. at beg. of next
12 (12: 12: 12: 14) rows, and 6 (8: 4:
6: 9) sts. at beg. of next 2 rows.
Leave rem. 44 (46: 48: 50: 52) sts. on a
holder.

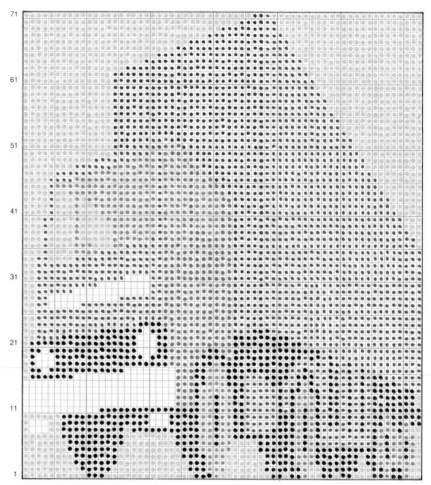

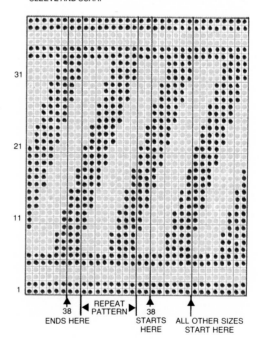

SLEEVE AND SCARF

REPEAT PATTERN
38 ENDS HERE
38 STARTS HERE
ALL OTHER SIZES START HERE

FRONT

Work as given for back until work measures 8½ (9½: 10½: 11½: 13) in., 22 (24: 27: 29: 33) cm. from beg. ending with a P row.

Next row – K25 (28: 31: 34: 38) sts. K 1st row of patt. from chart, K to end of row.

Next row – P26 (29: 32: 35: 39) sts., P 2nd row of patt. from chart, P to end of row.

Cont. working rows of patt. from chart as placed.

At the same time when work measures same as back to armholes, shape armholes.

○ To shape armholes

Inc. 1 st. at both ends of next and every foll. 10th row, 6 times. At the same time when work measures 18½ (19½: 20½: 21½: 23) in., 47 (49: 52: 55: 59) cm from beg. shape neck.

○ To shape neck

With RS work facing K51 (53: 55: 57: 62) sts, turn, leave rem. sts. on a spare needle. * Dec. 1 st. at neck edge on next 11 (11: 11: 11: 12) rows. Work straight until length measures same as back to shoulder, ending at armhole edge.

○ To shape shoulder

Cast off 6 (6: 7: 7: 6) sts at beg. of next and foll. 5 (5: 5: 5: 6) alt. rows. Work 1 row. Cast off 6 (8: 4: 6: 9) sts.
With RS work facing, sl. next 22 (24: 26: 28: 28) sts. onto a holder. Rejoin yarn to next st. and K to end of row. Complete to match first side from * to end.

SLEEVES

With 2¾mm needles and MC cast on 60 (60: 64: 64: 68) sts.
Work as given for back from ** to **.
On the last row inc. 44 (44: 48: 48: 48) sts. evenly. [104 (104: 112: 112: 116) sts].
Change to 3¼mm needles and starting with a K row work in st. st. Cont. straight until sleeve measures 10½ (11½: 12½: 13½: 13½) in, 27 (29: 32: 34: 34) cm. from beg. ending with a P row.
Join in contrast A and work sleeve patt. across all sts.
When patt. completed work 9 rows MC. Cast off.

POLO COLLAR

Sew up left shoulder seam.
With 2¾mm needles and MC pick up and K44 (46: 48: 50: 52) sts. from back neck, 22 (22: 22: 22: 24) sts from left side neck, 22 (24: 26: 28: 28) sts. from

centre front and 22 (22: 22: 22: 24) sts. from right side neck. [110 (114: 118: 122: 128) sts].
Work in K2 P2 rib for 4½in (11 cm).
Join in con A and work 3 rows, then 3 rows MC. Cast off loosely in rib.

TO MAKE UP

Press work according to yarn instructions omitting ribbing.
Sew up right shoulder and polo collar.
Sew in sleeves.
Sew up side and sleeve seams.

SCARF

MATERIALS

Yarn 3× 50g 4 ply main colour (yellow)
1 × 50g contrast A (black)
Needles 1 pair 3¼mm (UK 10)

MEASUREMENTS

Length 42 in (107 cm) excluding fringe
Width 6 in (15 cm)

INSTRUCTIONS

With 3¼mm needles and MC cast on 84 sts. Starting with a K row, work 10 rows in st. st.
*** Join in con A and work rows of sleeve patt. from chart across all sts, (starting and finishing where indicated for size 38 in (97 cm) sweater). ***
When patt. completed work a further 31 in (79 cm) in MC. Rep. from *** to *** once. Work 10 rows MC. Cast off.

TO MAKE UP

Press work according to yarn instructions. Join long edge together and placing seam at centre back, press again.
Sew on tassels, using 14 strands of yarn each 38 cm long, folded in half, for each tassel.

BEETLEMANIA

For those who prefer smaller vehicles, here's a jolly jumper featuring a favourite car.

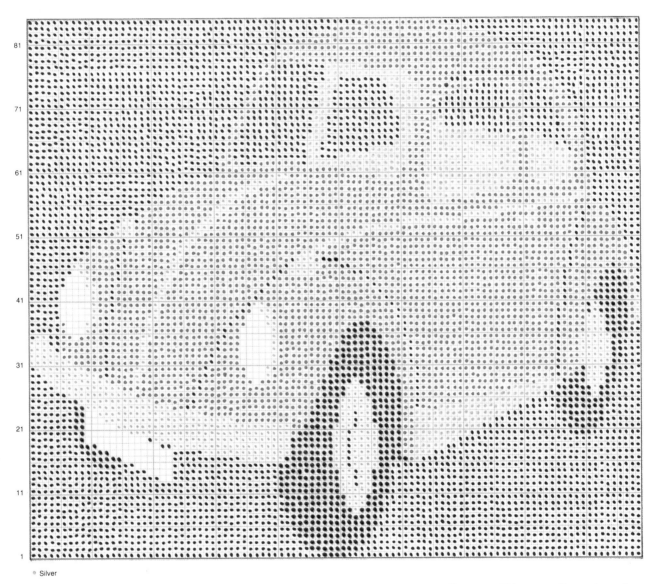

Silver

MATERIALS

Yarn 7 (7: 8: 8) × 50g 4 ply Main Colour (blue)
1 × 50g Contrast A – red
Small amounts Contrasts B – grey, C – silver, D – white
Needles 1 pair 2¾mm (UK 12)
1 pair 3¼mm (UK 10)

MEASUREMENTS

To fit chest 32 (34: 36: 38) in, 82 (87: 92: 97) cm
Length 22½ (23½: 24½: 25½) in, 57 (60: 62: 65) cm

Sleeve seam 18 (18: 19: 19) in, 46 (46: 48: 48) cm.

TENSION

28 sts and 36 rows to 10 cm square on 3¼mm needles (or size needed to obtain given tension).

BACK

With 2¾mm needles and MC cast on 120 (126: 130: 138) sts.
Working in K2 P2 rib, work 2 rows MC, 3 rows Con A, then 2 in. (5 cm) in MC.

Change to 3¼mm needles and starting with a K row, work in st. st. Cont. straight until work measures 13½ (14½: 15½: 16½) in. 34 (37: 39: 42) cm. from beg. ending with a P row.

○ To shape armholes

*Dec. 1 st. at both ends on next and foll. 6 alt. rows [106 (112: 116: 124) sts]. * Work straight until armhole measures 9 in (23 cm).

○ To shape shoulders

Cast off 6 (7: 7: 7) sts at beg. of next 8 rows, and 6 (4: 5: 8) sts. at beg. of next 2 rows.
Leave rem. 46 (48: 50: 52) sts on a holder.

FRONT

Work as given for back until work measures 6½ (7½: 8½: 9½) in, 16 (19: 22: 24) cm from beg. ending with a P row.

Next row – K10 (13: 15: 19) sts., K 1st row of patt. from chart, K to end of row.

Next row – P11 (14: 16: 20) sts. P 2nd row of patt. from chart, P to end of row.

Cont. working rows of patt. from chart as placed. At the same time when work measures same as back to armholes, shape armholes.

○ To shape armholes

Work as given for back from * to * keeping patt. over central sts. as set. Work straight until armhole measures 6 in (15 cm).

○ To shape neck

With RS work facing K42 (44: 45: 48) sts, turn, leave rem. sts. on a spare needle.

** Dec. 1 st. at neck edge on the next 12 rows. Work straight until length measures same as back to shoulder, ending at armhole edge.

○ To shape shoulder

Cast off 6 (7: 7: 7) sts at beg. of next and foll. 3 alt. rows.

Work 1 row. Cast off 6 (4: 5: 8) sts. With RS of work facing, slip next 22 (24: 26: 28) sts onto a holder. Rejoin yarn to next st. and K to end of row. Complete to match first side from ** to end.

SLEEVES

With 2¾mm needles and MC cast on 64 (64: 68: 68) sts.

Working in K2 P2 rib, work 2 rows MC, 3 rows Con A, then 2 in. (5 cm) in MC.

Change to 3¼mm needles and starting with a K row, work in st. st. Inc. 1 st. at both ends on the next and every foll. 4th row until 132 sts. Work straight until sleeve measures 18 (18: 19: 19) in, 46 (46: 48: 48) cm from beg. ending with a P row.

○ To shape top

Dec. 1 st. at both ends on next and foll. 6 alt. rows. [118 sts]. Work 1 row. Cast off.

NECKBAND

Sew up left shoulder seam.

With 2¾mm needles and MC pick up and K46 (48: 50: 52) sts. from back neck, 24 sts from left side neck, 22 (24: 26: 28) sts. from centre front and 24 sts from right side neck. [116 (120: 124:

128) sts]. Working in K2 P2 rib, work 5 rows MC, 3 rows Con A, 10 rows MC. Cast off loosely in rib.

TO MAKE UP

Press work according to yarn instructions omitting ribbing.
Sew up right shoulder and neckband.

Fold neckband in half and sew down on wrong side.
Sew in sleeves. Sew up side and sleeve seams.

ONTHETRACK

A power-packed Formula One sweater for a budding race ace.

MATERIALS

Yarn 4 (4: 5: 5: 6) × 50g 4 ply main colour (white)
3 (3: 3: 4: 4) × 50g – Contrast A (red)
2 (2: 2: 3: 3) × 50g – Contrast B (black)
1 × 50g – Contrast C (yellow)
Small amounts Contrasts D – wine, E – silver, F – blue, G – grey.
Needles 1 pair 2¾mm (UK 12)
1 pair 3¼mm (UK 10)

MEASUREMENTS

To fit bust/chest 30 (32: 34: 36: 38) in, 76 (81: 87: 92: 97) cm.
Length 20½ (21½: 22½: 23½: 25½) in, 52 (55: 57: 60: 65) cm.
Sleeve seam 16 (17: 18: 19: 19) in, 41 (43: 46: 48: 48) cm

TENSION

28 sts and 36 rows to 10 cm square on 3¼mm needles (or size needed to obtain given tension).

STRIPE PATTERN 1

(in K2 P2 rib)
6 rows A, 2 rows B, 10 rows C, 2 rows B, 6 rows A.

STRIPE PATTERN 2

(in K2 P2 rib)
2 rows A, 2 rows B, 4 rows C, 2 rows B, 13 rows A.

STRIPE PATTERN 3

1 row B, 2 rows C, 1 row B.

BACK

With 2¾mm needles and Con A cast on 114 (120: 126: 132: 140) sts.
Work *Stripe patt.* 1.
Change to 3¼mm needles and MC, and starting with a K row, work in st. st.
Cont. straight until work measures 13½ (14½: 15½: 16½: 18) in, 34 (37: 39: 42: 46) cm. from beg. ending with a P row.

○ To shape armholes
Inc. 1 st. at both ends of next and every foll. 10th row, 6 times, [128 (134: 140: 146: 154) sts]. Work 5 (5: 5: 5: 7) rows straight.

○ To shape shoulders
Cast off 6 (6: 7: 7: 6) sts at beg. of next 12 (12: 12: 12: 14) rows, and 6 (8: 4: 6: 9) sts. at beg. of next 2 rows.

Leave rem. 44 (46: 48: 50: 52) sts on a holder.

FRONT

Work as given for back until work measures 10 (11: 12: 13: 14½) in, 25 (28: 30: 33: 37) cm. from beg. ending with a P row.
Next row – K13 (16: 19: 22: 26) sts, K 1st row of patt. from chart, K to end of row.
Next row – P3 (6: 9: 12: 16) sts, P 2nd row of patt. from chart, P to end of row.

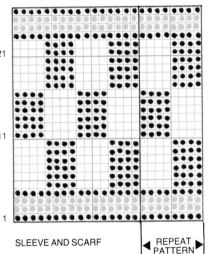

SLEEVE AND SCARF   ◀ REPEAT PATTERN ▶

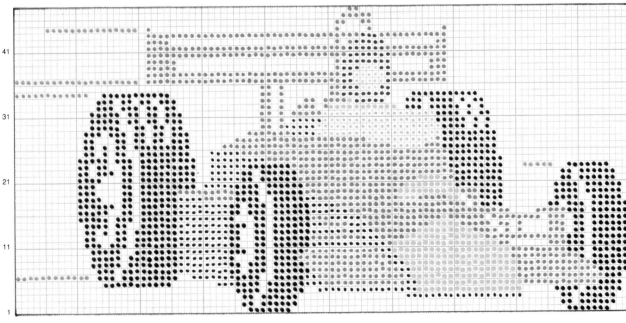

Silver

Cont. working rows of patt. from chart as placed. At the same time when work measures same as back to armholes, shape armholes.

○ To shape armholes
Inc. 1 st. at both ends of next and every foll. 10th row 6 times. At the same time when work measures 18½ (19½: 20½: 21½: 23) in., 47 (49: 52: 55: 59) cm. from beg. shape neck.

○ To shape neck
With RS work facing K51 (53: 55: 57: 62) sts, turn, leave rem. sts on a spare needle. * Dec. 1 st. at neck edge on next 11 (11: 11: 11: 12) rows. Work straight until length measures same as back to shoulder, ending at armhole edge.

○ To shape shoulder
Cast off 6 (6: 7: 7: 6) sts at beg. of next and foll. 5 (5: 5: 5: 6) alt. rows. Work 1 row.
Cast off 6 (8: 4: 6: 9) sts.
With RS work facing, sl. next 22 (24: 26: 28: 28) sts. onto a holder. Rejoin yarn to next st. and K to end of row. Complete to match first side from * to end.

SLEEVES

With 2¾mm needles and Con. A cast on 60 (60: 64: 64: 68) sts.
Work *Stripe patt* 1. On the last row inc. 44 (44: 48: 48: 52) sts. evenly [104 (104: 112: 112: 120) sts].
Change to 3¼mm needles and starting with a K row work in st. st. Cont. straight until sleeve measures 9½ (10½: 11½: 12½: 12½) in., 24 (27: 29: 32: 32) cm. from beg. ending with a P row.
Work rows of *Stripe Patt* 3., then work chequers patt. as follows.
** *1st row* – * K4 MC, K4 B, rep from * to end.
2nd row – * P4 B, P4 MC, rep from * to end.
Rep. last 2 rows twice more.
7th row – K4 B, K4 MC, rep from * to end.
8th row – * P4 MC, P4 B, rep. from * to end.
Rep. last 2 rows twice more, then first 2 rows 3 times. (18 rows in all). **
Work rows of *Stripe patt* 3. Rejoin Con. A and work 8 rows. Break off A and work 3 rows MC. Cast off.

NECKBAND

Sew up left shoulder seam.
With 2¾mm needles and Con. A pick up and K44 (46: 48: 50: 52) sts from back neck, 22 (22: 22: 22: 24) sts. from left side neck, 22 (24: 26: 28: 28) sts. from centre front and 22 (22: 22: 22: 24) sts, from right side neck. [110 (114: 118: 122: 128) sts]. Work rows of *Stripe patt*. 2.

Cast off loosely in rib.

TO MAKE UP

Press work according to yarn instructions, omitting ribbing.
Sew up right shoulder and neckband. Fold neckband in half and sew down on wrong side. Sew in sleeves. Sew up side and sleeve seams.

SCARF

MATERIALS

Yarn 1 × 50g Main Colour (white)
3 × 50g 4 ply – Contrast A (red)
1 × 50g Contrast B (black)
Small amount Contrast C – yellow.
Needles 1 pair 3¼mm (UK 10)

MEASUREMENTS

Length 42 in (107 cm) excluding fringe

Width 6½ in (16 cm)

INSTRUCTIONS

With 3¼mm needles and Con. A cast on 88 sts. Starting with a K row, work 2 in. (5 cm) in st. st. ending with a P row.
*** Work rows of *Stripe patt* 3. Work chequers patt. as for sleeve, rep. rows from ** to ** twice (36 rows in all). Work rows of *Stripe patt* 3. ***
Rejoin Con A and work a further 28 in (71 cm) ending with a P row.
Rep. from *** to ***. Rejoin in Con A and work 2 in. (5 cm) Cast off.

TO MAKE UP

Press work according to yarn instructions. Join long edge together and placing seam at centre back press again.
Sew on tassels, using 14 strands of yarn each 38 cm long, folded in half, for each tassel.

TOUCHDOWN!

Support your favourite team in this sporty American football sweater.

MATERIALS

Yarn 8 (8: 9: 9) × 50g 4 ply main colour (black)
2 (2: 3: 3) × 50g Contrast A (white)
1 × 50g Contrast B (red)
Small amounts Contrasts C – blue, D – yellow.
Needles 1 pair 2¾mm (UK 12)
1 pair 3¼mm (UK 10)

MEASUREMENTS

To fit bust/chest 32 (34: 36: 38) in, 81 (87: 92: 97) cm
Length 25½ in, 65cm
Sleeve seam 17½ (17½: 18: 18½) in, 44 (44: 46: 47) cm.

TENSION

28 sts and 36 rows to 10 cm square on 3¼mm needles (or size needed to obtain given tension).

STRIPE PATTERN 1

(in K2 P2 rib)
2 rows MC, 2 rows B, 2 rows MC, 4 rows A, 2 rows MC, 2 rows C, 2 rows MC, 4 rows A, 2 rows MC, 2 rows B.

STRIPE PATTERN 2

2 rows B, 2 rows MC, 10 rows A, 2 rows MC, 4 rows C, 2 rows MC, 10 rows A, 2 rows MC, 2 rows B.

STRIPE PATTERN 3

(in K2 P2 rib)
2 rows MC, 2 rows B, 2 rows A, 2 rows C, 2 rows A, 2 rows B, 14 rows MC.

BACK

With 2¾mm needles and MC cast on 106 (112: 120: 126) sts.
Work rows of *Stripe patt.* 1. Rejoin MC.
Change to 3¼mm needles and starting with a K row, work in st. st. At the same time inc. 1 st. at both ends on next and every foll. 10th row until 132 (138: 146: 152) sts.
Work 1 row.

○ **To shape armholes**
*Dec. 1 st. (3 stitches from edge) at both ends on next and foll. 6 alt. rows. [118 (124: 132: 138) sts]. * Work straight until armhole measures 10 in (25 cm), ending with a P row.

○ **To shape shoulders**
Cast off 7 (7: 8: 8) sts. at beg. of next 8 rows, and 6 (8: 7: 9) sts. at beg. next 2 rows.
Leave rem. 50 (52: 54: 56) sts on a holder.

FRONT

Work as given for back until work measures 11 in (28 cm) from beg. ending with a P row. [124 (130: 138: 144) sts].
Next row – K25 (28: 32: 35) sts., K. 1st row of patt. from chart, K to end of row.
Next row – P26 (29: 33: 36) sts, P. 2nd row of patt. from chart, P to end of row.
Cont. working rows of patt. from chart as placed, and inc. 1 st. at both ends of every 10th row as before, to 132 (138: 146: 152) sts. Work 1 row.

○ **To shape armholes**
Work as given for back from * to *, keeping patt. as set. Work straight until armhole measures 8 in (20 cm).

○ **To shape neck**
With RS facing K47 (49: 52: 54) sts, turn, leave rem. sts on a spare needle.
** Dec. 1 st. at neck edge on the next 13 rows. Work straight until length measures same as back to shoulder, ending at armhole edge.

○ **To shape shoulder**
Cast off 7 (7: 8: 8) sts at beg. of next and foll. 3 alt. rows.
Work 1 row. Cast off 6 (8: 7: 9) sts.
With RS work facing sl. next 24 (26: 28: 30) sts. onto a holder. Rejoin yarn to next st. and K to end of row.
Complete to match first side from ** to end.

SLEEVES

With 2¾mm needles and MC cast on 64 sts, and work rows of *Stripe patt.* 1.
Rejoin MC. Change to 3¼mm needles

and starting with a K row, work in st. st.
Inc. 1 st. at both ends on next and foll. 11 alt. rows [88 sts], then every foll. 4th row until there are 140 sts.
At the same time when sleeve measures 12½ (12½: 13: 13½) in, 32 (32: 33: 34) cm from beg. ending with a P row, work rows of *Stripe patt 2.*
When shaping completed work straight until sleeve measures 17½ (17½: 18: 18½) in. 44 (44: 46: 47) cm from beg. ending with a P row.

○ **To shape top**
Dec 1 st. at both ends on next and foll. 6 alt. rows. [126 sts]. Work 1 row. Cast off.

NECKBAND

Sew up left shoulder.
With 2¾mm needles and MC, pick up and K50 (52: 54: 56) sts from back neck, 26 sts. from left side neck, 24 (26: 28: 30) sts from centre front and 26 sts. from right side neck [126 (130: 134: 138) sts.] Work rows of *Stripe patt 3.*
Cast off loosely in rib.

TO MAKE UP

Press work according to yarn instructions, omitting ribbing.
Sew up right shoulder and neckband.
Fold neckband in half and sew down on wrong side.
Sew in sleeves. Sew up side and sleeve seams.

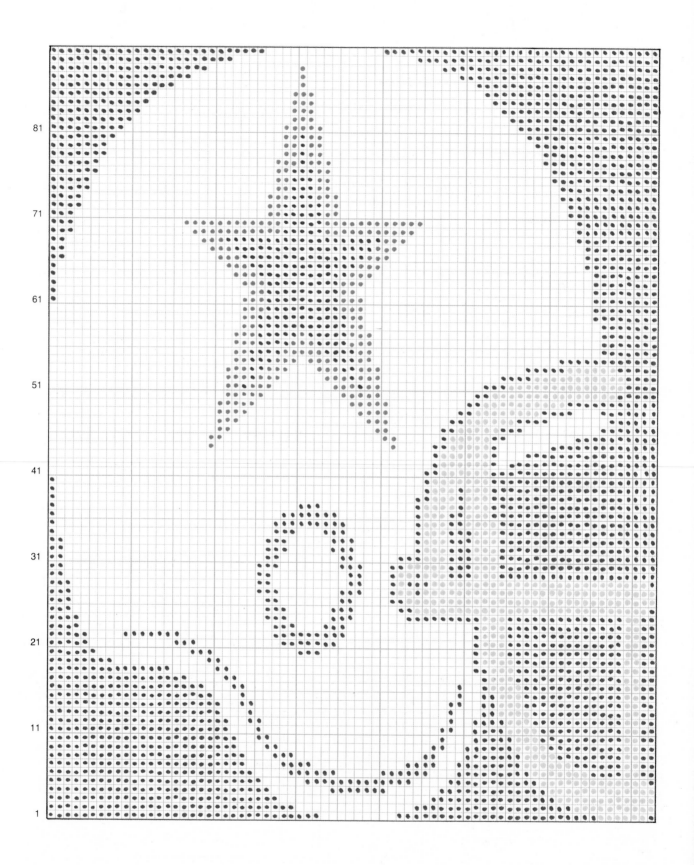

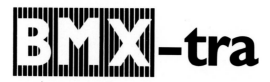

BMX-tra

Get on your bike with this snazzy BMX jumper

MATERIALS

Yarn 4 (4: 4: 5: 5) × 50g 4 ply (yellow) main colour
1 × 50g Contrast A (red)
2 × 50g Contrast B (yellow)
1 × 25g Contrast C (silver)
Needles 1 pair 2¾mm (UK 12)
1 pair 3¼mm (UK 10)

MEASUREMENTS

To fit chest 28 (30: 32: 34: 36) in. 71 (76: 81: 87: 92) cm
Length 19½ (20½: 21½: 22½: 23½) in. 49 (52: 55: 57: 60) cm
Sleeve seam 15 (16: 17: 18: 19) in. 38 (41: 43: 46: 48) cm

TENSION

28 sts and 36 rows to 10 cm square on 3¼mm needles (or size needed to obtain given tension).

STRIPE PATTERN 1

4 rows MC, 2 rows A, 6 rows B, 2 rows A, 4 rows MC.

STRIPE PATTERN 2

3 rows MC, 2 rows A, 4 rows B, 2 rows A, 13 rows MC.

STRIPE PATTERN 3

2 rows A, 2 rows C, 2 rows A, ★ 5 rows B, 2 rows C, 4 rows MC ★ rep from ★ to ★ twice more, 5 rows B, 2 rows A, 2 rows C, 2 rows A.

STRIPE PATTERN 4

★ 2 rows A, 2 rows C, 2 rows A ★, 39 rows MC, rep from ★ to ★ once.

BACK

With 2¾mm needles and MC cast on 108 (114: 120: 126: 132) sts.
Working in K2 P2 rib, work rows of *Stripe patt.* 1.

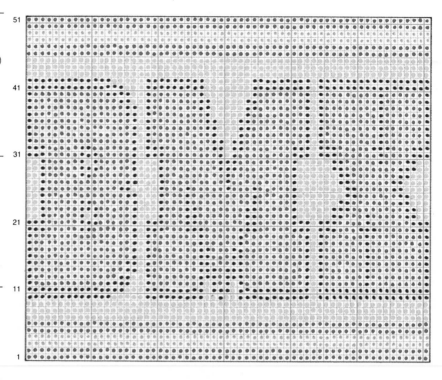

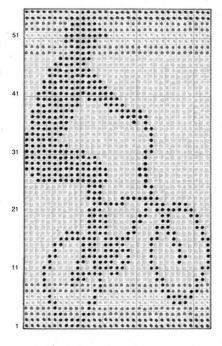

Change to 3¼mm needles and starting with a K row work in st. st.
Cont. straight until work measures 5½ (6½: 7½: 8½: 9½] in, 14 (16: 19: 22: 24) cm. from beg. ending with a P row. ★★ Work rows of *Stripe patt* 4. Rejoin MC and cont. straight until work measures 12½ (13½: 14½: 15½: 16½) in, 32 (34: 37: 39: 42) cm. from beg. ending with a P row.

○ To shape armholes

Inc 1 st. at both ends of next and every foll. 10th row, 6 times [122 (128: 134: 140: 146) sts.]. Work 5 rows straight.

○ To shape shoulders

Cast off 6 (6: 6: 7: 7) sts at beg. next 12 rows, and 4 (6: 8: 4: 6) sts. at beg. of next 2 rows.
Leave rem 42 (44: 46: 48: 50) sts. on a holder.

FRONT

Work as given for back to ★★. Joining in contrasts where necessary commence patt. 1 from chart as follows.
Work rows 1–9 (inclusive) across all sts. of the front.
10th row – P23 (26: 29: 32: 35) sts., P 10th row of patt. from chart, P to end of row.

11th row – K24 (27: 30: 33: 36) sts, K 11th row of patt. from chart, K to end of row.
Cont. working rows of patt. from chart as placed to row 45.
Rows 46–51 (inclusive), work across all sts of the front.
When patt. completed rejoin MC and cont. straight until work measures same as back to armholes ending with a P row.

○ To shape armholes
Inc. 1 st. at both ends of next and every foll. 10th row, 6 times. At the same time when work measures 17½ (18½: 19½: 20½: 21½) in, 44 (47: 49: 52: 55) cm, from beg. shape neck.

○ To shape neck
With RS work facing K49 (51: 53: 55: 57) sts, turn, leave rem. sts on a spare needle. * Dec 1 st. at neck edge on the next 11 rows.
Work straight until length measures same as back to shoulder, ending at armhole edge.

○ To shape shoulder
Cast off 6 (6: 6: 7: 7) sts at beg. of next and foll. 5 alt rows.
Work 1 row. Cast off 4 (6: 8: 4: 6) sts.
With RS work facing sl. next 20 (22: 24: 26: 28) sts. onto a holder.
Rejoin yarn to next st. and K to end of row. Complete to match first side from * to end.

LEFT SLEEVE

With 2¾mm needles and MC cast on 56 (60: 60: 64: 64) sts.
Work rows of *Stripe patt* 1 in K2 P2 rib, on the last row inc. 42 (44: 44: 48: 48) sts evenly. [98 (104: 104: 112: 112) sts].
Change to 3¼mm needles and starting with a K row, work in st. st. *
Cont. straight until work measures 8½ (9½: 10½: 11½: 12½) in, 22 (24: 27: 29: 32) cm from beg. ending with a P row.
Joining in contrasts where necessary work rows of *Stripe patt* 3.
** Rejoin MC and cont. straight until work measures 15 (16: 17: 18: 19) in, 38 (41: 43: 46: 48) cm. from beg. Cast off.

RIGHT SLEEVE

Work as for left sleeve to *. Cont. straight until work measures 8 (9: 10: 11: 12) in, 20 (23: 25: 28: 30) cm from beg. ending with a P row.
Next row – K33 (36: 36: 40: 40) sts, K 1st row of patt. 2 from chart. K to end of row.
Next row – P32 (35: 35: 39: 39) sts, P 2nd row of patt 2. from chart. P to end of row.
Cont. working rows of patt. from chart

as placed, working the stripe rows across all sts.
When patt. completed rejoin MC and complete as for left sleeve from ** to end.

NECKBAND

Sew up left shoulder seam.
With 2¾mm needles and MC pick up and K42 (44: 46: 48: 50) sts from back neck, 22 sts from left side neck, 20 (22: 24: 26: 28) sts. from centre front and 22 sts from right side neck. [106 (110: 114: 118: 122) sts].
Work rows of *Stripe patt.* 2 in K2 P2 rib. Cast off loosely in rib.

TO MAKE UP

Press work according to yarn instructions, omitting ribbing.
Sew up right shoulder and neckband.
Fold neckband in half and sew down on wrong side.
Sew in sleeves. Sew up side and sleeve seams.

SNOWSTORM

For Arctic weather – a big cuddly sweater to snuggle into.

MATERIALS

Yarn 9 (9: 10: 10) × 50g Pingouin Orage Main Colour – (red)
3 (3: 4: 4) × 50g Contrast A – white.
Needles 1 pair 4½mm (UK 7)
1 pair 5 mm (UK 6)
Set of 4 needles size 4½mm (UK 7)

MEASUREMENTS

To fit bust/chest 26 (28: 30: 32) in, 66 (71: 76: 81) cm (fits loosely)
Length 24 (24: 25¼: 25¼) in, 61 (61: 64: 64) cm
Sleeve seam 17 (17: 18½: 18½) in, 43 (43: 47: 47) cm.

TENSION

16 sts and 22 rows to 10 cm square on 5 mm needles (or size needed to obtain given tension).

SPECIAL ABBREVIATION

Bobble – make bobble as follows: (K1, P1, K1, P1) into next st., turn, P4, turn, K4, turn, (P2tog) twice, turn, K2tog.

BACK

With 4½mm needles and MC cast on 76 (80: 86: 90) sts.
Work in K1, P1, rib for 2 in., (5 cm).
Change to 5mm needles and starting with a K row, work 6 rows in st. st.
Joining in Con A where necessary commence bobble patt. as follows.
1st row – K8 (10: 8: 10) sts, * bobble, K9, * rep from * to * 5 (5: 6: 6) times more, bobble, K7 (9: 7: 9).
2nd row – Purl
3rd row – Knit.
Rep. 2nd and 3rd rows 4 times, then 2nd row again.
13th row – K3 (5: 3: 5) sts, * bobble, K9, * rep from * to * 6 (6: 7: 7) times more, bobble, K2 (4: 2: 4).
Rep 2nd and 3rd rows 5 times.
24th row – Purl.
From 1st to 24th row (inclusive) forms patt. Keeping continuity of patt. (throughout) cont. until work measures 13¾ in, (35 cm) from beg. ending with a P row.

○ To shape armholes

Cast off 2 sts at beg. of next 4 rows, then 1 st. at beg. of next 2 rows. [66 (70: 76: 80) sts]. **
Cont. straight until work measures 24 (24: 25¼: 25¼) in, 61 (61: 64: 64) cm from beg. ending with a P row.

○ To shape shoulders

Cast off 15 (17: 19: 21) sts, K36 (36: 38: 38) sts and leave on a holder, cast off rem. 15 (17: 19: 21) sts.

FRONT

Work as given for back to **. Cont. straight until work measures 22½ (22½: 23½: 23½) in, 57 (57: 60: 60) cm from beg. ending with a P row.

○ To shape neck

K27 (29: 32: 34) sts for left side neck and leave these sts on a spare needle. Cast off 12 sts, K. rem 27 (29: 32: 34) sts.
Cont. on last set of sts as follows.
Work 1 row.
Cast off 3 (3: 4: 4) sts at beg. of next row, then 3 sts. at beg. of foll. 3 alt. rows. [15 (17: 19: 21) sts].
Work straight until length measures same as back to shoulder, ending with a P row. Cast off.
With WS work facing rejoin yarn to rem. sts at neck edge and complete to match first side reversing all shapings.

SLEEVES

With 4½mm needles and MC cast on 30 (30: 34: 34) sts.
Work in K1, P1 rib for 2½ in (6 cms).
On the last row inc. 10 sts evenly. [40 (40: 44: 44) sts].
Change to 5mm needles and starting with a K row, work in st. st.
Inc. 1 st. at both ends of next and foll alt. rows 2 (2: 5: 5) times, then every 4th row until 82 (82: 92: 92) sts. At the same time work bobble patt. as follows:
7th row – K8 (8: 5: 5) sts, * bobble, K9, * rep. from * to *, 2 (2: 3: 3) times more, bobble, K 7 (7: 4: 4).
Work 11 rows.
19th row – K6 (6: 4: 4) sts, * bobble, K9, * rep. from * to * 3 (3: 4: 4) times more, bobble, K5 (5: 3: 3).
Keeping continuity of patt. as set, work extra sts. in patt.

When shaping completed cont. straight until sleeve measures 17 (17: 18½: 18½) in., 43 (43: 47: 47) cm, from beg. ending with a P row.

○ To shape top

Cast off 9 (9: 10: 10) sts at beg. of next 6 rows. [28 (28: 32: 32) sts]. Cast off loosely.

POLO NECK COLLAR

Sew shoulder seams.
With set of 4½mm needles and Con A, pick up and K17 sts down left side of front neck, 12 sts from centre front, 17 sts up right side of front neck and 36 (36: 38: 38) sts. from back neck. [82 (82: 84: 84) sts]. Work in rounds of K1, P1 rib for 8 in. (20 cm). Cast off loosely in rib.

TO MAKE UP

Press work according to yarn instructions, omitting ribbing.
Sew in sleeves. Sew up side and sleeve seams.

PICK A P-PENGUIN

And for Antarctic weather – a fun way to get the bird.

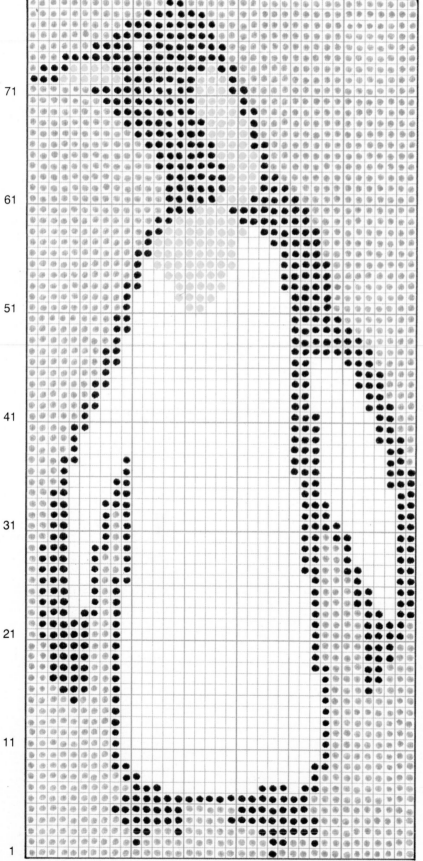

MATERIALS

Yarn 6 (6: 7: 7) × 50g balls Pingouin Kirouna main colour (grey)
1 × 50g white, black, yellow.
Needles 1 pair 4½mm (UK 7)
1 pair 5mm (UK 6)

MEASUREMENTS

To fit chest 26 (28: 32: 34) in, 66 (71: 81: 86) cms
Length 17½ (18½: 21¼: 23) in, 44 (47: 54: 58) cm.
Sleeve seam 12½ (14: 16½: 19) in, 32 (36: 42: 48) cm

TENSION

20 sts and 24 rows to 10 cm square on 5mm needles (or size needed to obtain given tension).

BACK

With 4½mm needles cast on 72 (72: 92: 92) sts. Work in K1, P1, rib for 1¾ in., (4 cm). On the last row inc. 8 sts evenly. [80 (80: 100: 100) sts].
Change to 5mm needles and starting with a K row, work in st. st.★
Cont. straight until work measures 10½ (11½: 13½: 14½) in., 27 (29: 34: 37) cm. from beg. ending with a P row.

○ **To shape armholes**
Cast off 6 sts. at beg. next 2 rows. [68 (68: 88: 88) sts].
Cont. straight until work measures 17½ (18½: 21¼: 23) in., 44 (47: 54: 58) cm, from beg. ending with a purl row.

○ **To shape shoulders and neck**
Cast off 6 (5: 7: 6) sts. at beg. next 2 rows and 0 (0: 6: 6) sts at beg. foll. 2 rows.
Next row – Cast off 6 sts, K6 sts (incl. st. on needle), turn.
Next row – P.
Next row – Cast off 6 sts.
With RS work facing sl. next 32 (34: 38: 40) sts onto a holder.
Rejoin yarn to next st. and K to end.
Next row – Cast off 6 sts. P to end.
Work 1 row. Cast off rem. sts.

FRONT

Work as for back to * Cont. straight until work measures 2 (2½: 4: 4¾) in., 5 (6: 10: 12) cm from beg. ending with a P row.

Next row – K21 (21: 31: 31) sts. K 1st row of patt. from chart, K to end of row.

Next row – P22 (22: 32: 32) sts. P 2nd row of patt. from chart, P to end of row.

Cont. working rows of patt. from chart as placed, at the same time when work measures same as back to armholes, ending with a P row, shape armholes.

○ To shape armholes

Cast off 6 sts at beg. next 2 rows [68 (68: 88: 88) sts].

Cont. straight until work measures 15½ (16½: 19½: 20½) in., 39 (42: 49: 52) cm. from beg. ending with a P row.

○ To shape neck

With RS work facing K28 (27: 36: 35) sts., turn, leaving rem. sts on a spare needle.

** Cast off at neck edge on next and foll. alt. rows, 3 sts once, 2 sts twice and 1 st. 3 (3: 4: 4) times.

Cont. straight until work measures same as back to shoulder, ending at armhole edge.

○ To shape shoulder

Cast off 6 (5: 7: 6) sts at beg. next row, and 0 (0: 6: 6) sts at beg. foll. alt. row. Work 1 row.

Cast off 6 sts. at beg. next and foll. alt row.

With RS work facing, slip next 12 (14: 16: 18) sts onto a holder.

Rejoin yarn to neck st. and complete to match first side from ** to end.

SLEEVES

With 4½mm needles cast on 40 (40: 46: 50) sts. Work in K1, P1 rib for 1¾ in., (4 cm). On the last row inc. 8 sts evenly. [48 (48: 54: 58) sts].

Change to 5mm and starting with a K row work in st. st.

Inc. 1 st. at both ends of the 6th and every foll. 6 (6: 6: 8)th row until there are 68 (72: 80: 84) sts.

Cont. straight until sleeve measures 12½ (14: 16½: 19) in., 32 (36: 42: 48) cms, from beg. Cast off.

NECKBAND

Join left shoulder.

With RS work facing and 4½mm needles, pick up and K3 sts down right back slope, 32 (34: 38: 40) sts. from back neck, 3 sts up left back slope, 20 sts. down left front neck, 12 (14: 16: 18) sts from centre front and 20 sts. up right front neck. [90 (94: 100: 104) sts].

Work in K1, P1, rib for 1¾ in., (4 cms). Cast off loosely in rib.

TO MAKE UP

Press work according to yarn instructions omitting ribbing.
Sew up right shoulder and neckband.
Fold neckband in half and sew down on wrong side. Sew in sleeves. Sew up side and sleeve seams.

MIAOOOWWW!

Vivid stripes and a psychedelic cat adorn this exciting sweater and scarf.

SWEATER

MATERIALS

Yarn 5 (5: 6: 7: 7) × 50g 4 ply main colour (blue)
2 × 50g Contrast A – black
Small amounts Contrasts B – fuchsia, C – yellow, D – red.
Needles 1 pair 2¾mm (UK 12)
1 pair 3¼mm (UK 10)

MEASUREMENTS

To fit bust/chest 30 (32: 34: 36: 38) in., 76 (82: 87: 92: 97) cm.
Length 20½ (21½: 22½: 23½: 25½) in, 52 (55: 57: 60: 65) cm.
Sleeve seam 16 (17: 18: 19: 19) in., 41 (43: 46: 48: 48) cm.

TENSION

28 sts and 36 rows to 10 cm square on 3¼mm needles (or size needed to obtain given tension).

STRIPE PATTERN

4 rows A, 4 rows B, 4 rows A, 4 rows MC, 4 rows A, 4 rows MC, 4 rows A, 4 rows C, 4 rows A.

BACK

With 2¾mm needles and MC cast on 114 (120: 126: 132: 140) sts.
Work in K2 P2 rib. for 2½ in (6 cm).
Change to 3¼mm needles and starting with a K row, work in st. st. Cont. straight until work measures 13½ (14½: 15½: 16½: 18) in, 34 (37: 39: 42: 46) cm from beg. ending with a P row.

○ To shape armholes
Inc. 1 st. at both ends of next and every foll. 10th row, 6 times, [128 (134: 140: 146: 154) sts]. Work 5 (5: 5: 5: 7) rows straight.

○ To shape shoulders
Cast off 6 (6: 7: 7: 6) sts. at beg. of next 12 (12: 12: 12: 14) rows, and 6 (8: 4: 6: 9) sts at beg. of next 2 rows.

Leave rem. 44 (46: 48: 50: 52) sts. on a holder.

FRONT

Work as given for back until work measures 5 (6: 7: 8: 9½) in, 13 (15: 18: 20: 24) cm. from beg. ending with a P row.
Next row – K21 (24: 27: 30: 34) sts, K 1st row of patt. from chart, K to end of row.
Next row – P22 (25: 28: 31: 35) sts, P 2nd row of patt. from chart, P to end of row.
Cont. working rows of patt. from chart as placed. At the same time when work measures same as back to armholes, shape armholes.

○ To shape armholes
Inc. 1 st. at both ends of next and every foll. 10th row, 6 times. At the same time when work measures 18½ (19½: 20½: 21½: 23) in, 47 (49: 52: 55: 59) cm from beg. shape neck.

○ To shape neck
With RS work facing K51 (53: 55: 57: 62) sts, turn, leave rem. sts on a spare needle. ★ Dec 1 st. at neck edge on next 11 (11: 11: 11: 12) rows. Work straight until length measures same as back to shoulder, ending at armhole edge.

○ To shape shoulder
Cast off 6 (6: 7: 7: 6) sts at beg. of next and foll. 5 (5: 5: 5: 6) alt. rows. Work 1 row. Cast off 6 (8: 4: 6: 9) sts.
With RS work facing, sl. next 22 (24: 26: 28: 28) sts. onto a holder. Rejoin yarn to next st. and K to end of row. Complete to match first side from ★ to end.

SLEEVES

With 2¾mm needles and MC cast on 60 (60: 64: 64: 68) sts.
Work in K2 P2 rib for 2¾ in (7 cm).
On the last row inc. 44 (44: 48: 48: 48) sts. evenly.
[104 (104: 112: 112: 116) sts].
Change to 3¼mm needles and starting with a K row, work rows of *Stripe patt.* in st. st.
Rejoin MC and working in st. st. cont. straight until work measures 16 (17: 18: 19: 19) in, 41 (43: 46: 48: 48) cm.

from beg.
Cast off.

NECKBAND

Sew up left shoulder seam.
With 2¾mm needles and MC pick up and K44 (46: 48: 50: 52) sts. from back neck, 22 (22: 22: 22: 24) sts. from left side neck, 22 (24: 26: 28: 28) sts. from centre front and 22 (22: 22: 22: 24) sts. from right side neck. [110 (114: 118: 122: 128) sts].
Work 2 in (5 cm) in K2, P2 rib.
Cast off loosely in rib.

TO MAKE UP

Press work according to yarn instructions, omitting ribbing.
Sew up right shoulder seam and neckband. Fold neckband in half and sew down on wrong side.
Sew in sleeves, sew up side and sleeve seams.

SCARF

MATERIALS

Yarn 3 × 50g 4 ply main colour (blue)
Small amounts – Contrasts A – black, B – fuchsia, C – yellow.
Needles 1 pair 3¼mm (UK 10)

MEASUREMENTS

Length 45½ in (116 cm) excluding fringe
Width 6 in (15 cm)

INSTRUCTIONS

With 3¼mm needles and MC cast on 84 sts.
Starting with a K row, work 10 rows in st. st.
Cont. in st. st. and work rows of *Stripe patt* as given for sweater sleeves.
Rejoin in MC and work a further 34½ in (88 cm), ending with a P row. Work rows of *Stripe patt*. then 10 rows in MC.
Cast off.

TO MAKE UP

Press work according to yarn
instructions. Join long edge together
and placing seam at centre back, press
again. Sew on tassels, using 14 strands
of yarn each 38 cm. long, folded in half,
for each tassel.

COMPUTER SCREEN

Glittering silver yarn gives a space-age look to this silicon-chip sweater.

MATERIALS

Yarn 6 (6: 7: 8) × 50g 4 ply main colour
(grey)
1 spool silver
2 × 50g Contrast A (white)
1 × 50g Contrast B (blue)
Small amounts Contrasts C – red, D –
yellow, E – green, F – pink.
Needles 1 pair 2¾mm (UK 12)
1 pair 3¼mm (UK 10)

MEASUREMENTS

To fit bust/chest 32 (34: 36: 38) in, 81
(87: 92: 97) cm
Length 25½ in, 65 cm
Sleeve seam 17½ (17½: 18: 18½) in,
44 (44: 46: 47) cm.

TENSION

28 sts and 36 rows to 10 cm square on
3¼mm needles (or size needed to
obtain given tension).

STRIPE PATTERN 1

(in K2, P2 rib)
3 rows MC, 4 rows B, 10 rows A, 4 rows
B, 3 rows MC.

STRIPE PATTERN 2

(in K2, P2, rib)
1 row MC, 2 rows B, 4 rows A, 2 rows
B, 11 rows MC.

SPECIAL NOTE

1 strand of 4 ply grey + 1 or 2 strands
of silver is referred to as main colour
(MC) throughout.

BACK

With 2¾mm needles and MC cast on
106 (112: 120: 126) sts.

Work rows of *Stripe patt. 1*.
Change to 3¼mm needles and starting
with a K row, work in st. st. At the
same time inc. 1 st. at both ends on next
and every foll. 10th row until 132 (138:
146: 152) sts.
Work 1 row.

○ To shape armholes
★ Dec. 1 st. (3 stitches from edge) at
both ends on next and foll. 6 alt. rows.
[118 (124: 132: 138) sts]. ★ Work
straight until armhole measures 10 in
(25 cm), ending with a P row.

○ To shape shoulders
Cast off 7 (7: 8: 8) sts. at beg. of next
8 rows, and 6 (8: 7: 9) sts. at beg. next
2 rows.
Leave rem. 50 (52: 54: 56) sts on a
holder.

FRONT

Work as given for back until work
measures 11 in (28 cm) from beg.
ending with a P row. [124 (130: 138:
144) sts].
Next row – K21 (24: 28: 31) sts., K 1st
row of patt. from chart, K to end of row.
Next row – P21 (24: 28: 31) sts, P 2nd
row of patt. from chart, P to end of
row.
Cont. working rows of patt. from chart
as placed, and inc. 1 st. at both ends
of every 10th row as before, to 132 (138:
146: 152) sts. Work 1 row.

○ To shape armholes
Work as given for back from ★ to ★,
keeping patt. as set. Work straight until
armhole measures 8in (20 cm.)

○ To shape neck
With RS facing K47 (49: 52: 54) sts,
turn, leave rem. sts on a spare needle.
★ ★ Dec. 1 st. at neck edge on the next
13 rows.
Work straight until length measures
same as back to shoulder, ending at
armhole edge.

○ To shape shoulder
Cast off 7 (7: 8: 8) sts. at beg. of next

and foll. 3 alt. rows. Work 1 row. Cast
off 6 (8: 7: 9) sts.
With RS work facing sl. next 24 (26:
28: 30) sts onto a holder. Rejoin yarn
to next st. and K to end of row.
Complete to match first side from ★ ★ to
end.

SLEEVES

With 2¾mm needles and MC cast on
64 sts and work rows of *Stripe patt* 1.
Change to 3¼mm needles and starting
with a K row, work in st. st.
Inc. 1 st. at both ends on next and foll.
11 alt. rows. [88 sts], then every foll.
4th row until there are 140 sts.
At the same time when work measures
12¼ (12¼: 12¾: 13¼) in, 31 (31: 32:
34) cm. from beg, ending with a P row,
break off MC. Joining in contrasts as
necessary work 4 rows Con B, 30 rows
Con A, and 4 rows Con B.
Rejoin MC and when shaping
completed work straight until sleeve
measures 17½ (17½: 18: 18½) in, 44
(44: 46: 47) cm. from beg. ending with
a P row.

○ To shape top
Dec. 1 st. at both ends on next and foll.
6 alt. rows. [126 sts]. Work 1 row. Cast
off.

NECKBAND

Sew up left shoulder.
With 2¾mm needles and MC pick up
and K50 (52: 54: 56) sts. from back
neck, 26 sts from left side neck, 24 (26:
28: 30) sts. from centre front and 26
sts from right side neck. [126 (130: 134:
138) sts]. Work rows of *Stripe patt*. 2.
Cast off loosely in rib.

TO MAKE UP

Press work according to yarn
instructions, omitting ribbing.
Sew up right shoulder and neckband.
Fold neckband in half and sew down
on wrong side. Sew in sleeves. Sew up
side and sleeve seams.

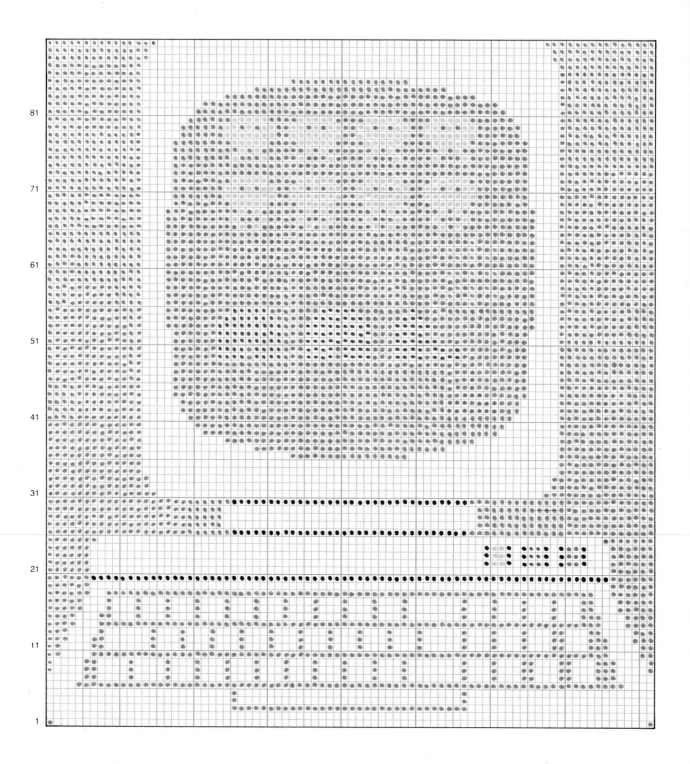

VIDEO MAN

An up-to-the-minute design for the boy or girl of the moment.

MATERIALS

Yarn 6 (7: 8: 9) × 50g 4 ply main colour (pale green)
1 × 50g Contrast A (yellow)
Small amounts Contrasts B – red, C – pink, D – dark blue, E – black.
Needles 1 pair 2¾mm (UK 12)
1 pair 3¼mm (UK 10)

MEASUREMENTS

To fit bust/chest 32 (34: 36: 38) in, 81 (87: 92: 97) cm
Length 26 in, 66 cm.
Sleeve seam 17½ (17½: 18: 18½) in, 44 (44: 46: 47) cm

TENSION

28 sts and 36 rows to 10 cm square on 3¼mm needles (or size needed to obtain given tension).

BACK

With 2¾mm needles and MC cast on 106 (112: 120: 126) sts.
Work in K2 P2 rib for 2½ in (6 cm). Change to 3¼mm needles and starting with a K row, work in st. st. At the same time inc. 1 st. at both ends on next and every foll. 10th row until 132 (138: 146: 152) sts. Work 1 row.

○ To shape armholes
* Dec. 1 st. (3 stitches from edge) at both ends on next and foll. 6 alt rows. [118 (124: 132: 138) sts]. * Work straight until armhole measures 10 in (25 cms) ending with a P row.

○ To shape shoulders
Cast off 7 (7: 8: 8) sts at beg. of next 8 rows, and 6 (7: 7: 9) sts. at beg. next 2 rows.
Leave rem. 50 (54: 54: 56) sts on a holder.

FRONT

Work as given for back until work measures 5 in (13 cm). from beg. ending with a P row. [112 (118: 126: 132) sts].
Next row – K10 (13: 17: 20) sts, K 1st row of patt. from chart, K to end of row.
Next row – P11 (14: 18: 21) sts, P 2nd row of patt. from chart, P to end of row.
Cont. working rows of patt. from chart as placed, and inc. 1 st. at both ends of every 10th row as before to 132 (138: 146: 152) sts. Work 1 row.

○ To shape armholes
Work as given for back from * to *, keeping patt. as set. Work straight until armhole measures 8 in (20 cm).

○ To shape neck
With RS facing, K47 (49: 53: 55) sts, turn, leave rem. sts. on a spare needle.
** Dec. 1 st. at neck edge on the next 13 (14: 14: 14) rows.
Work straight until length measures same as back to shoulder ending at armhole edge.

○ To shape shoulder
Cast off 7 (7: 8: 8) sts at beg. of next and foll. 3 alt. rows. Work 1 row. Cast off 6 (7: 7: 9) sts.
With RS work facing, slip next 24 (26: 26: 28) sts. onto a holder. Rejoin yarn to next st. and K to end of row.
Complete to match first side from ** to end.

SLEEVES

With 2¾mm needles cast on 64 sts and work 2¾ in (7 cm) in K2 P2 rib.
Change to 3¼mm needles and starting with a K row, work in st. st. At the same time inc. 1 st. at both ends on next and foll. 11 alt rows. [88 sts], then every foll. 4th row until there are 140 sts.
Work straight until sleeve measures 17½ (17½: 18: 18½) in, 44 (44: 46: 47) cm. from beg. ending with a P row.

○ To shape top
Dec. 1 st. at both ends on next and foll. 6 alt. rows. (126 sts). Work 1 row. Cast off.

ROLL NECKBAND

Sew up left shoulder.
With 3¼mm needles, pick up and K50 (54: 54: 56) sts. from back neck, 26 (28: 28: 28) sts. from left side neck, 24 (26: 26: 28) sts. from centre front and 26 (28: 28: 28) sts. from right side neck. [126 (136: 136: 140) sts.]. Starting with a P row, work 30 rows in rev. st. st. Cast off.

TO MAKE UP

Press work according to yarn instructions, omitting ribbing and roll neckband. Sew up right shoulder and neckband. Hold neckband in place with a few stitches at shoulder seams. Sew in sleeves. Sew up side and sleeve seams.

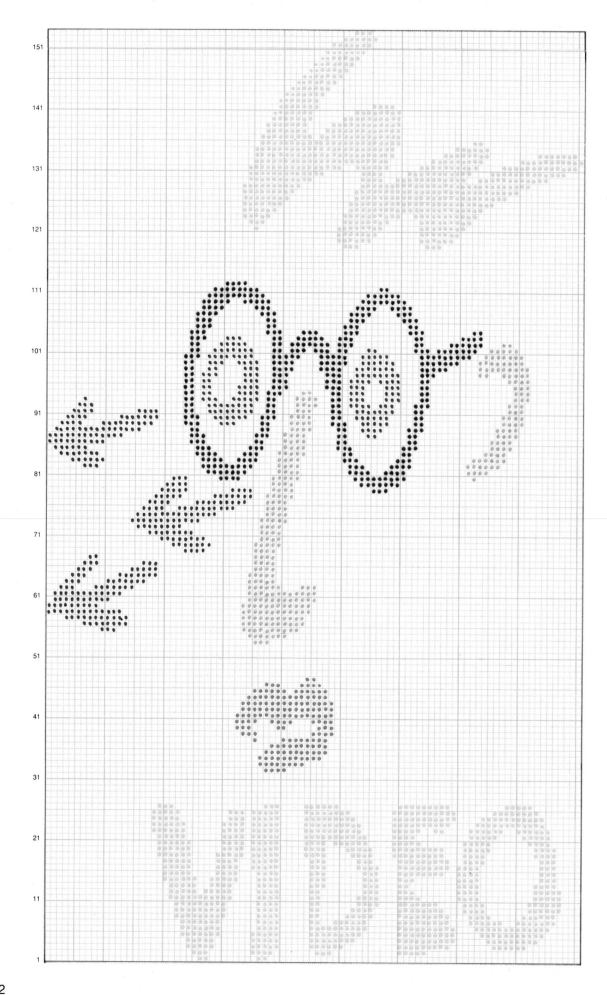

STEREO SOUND

A swinging sweater to give its wearer music wherever they go.

MATERIALS

Yarn 8 (8: 9: 9) × 50g 4 ply main colour (black)
1 × 50g Contrast A (yellow)
Small amounts Contrasts B – red, C – pale blue, D – grey, E – pink, F – dark blue.
Needles 1 pair 2¾mm (UK 12)
1 pair 3¼mm (UK 10)

MEASUREMENTS

To fit bust/chest 32 (34: 36: 38) in, 81 (87: 92: 97) cm
Length 25½ in, 65cm
Sleeve seam 17½ (17½: 18: 18½) in, 44 (44: 46: 47) cm.

TENSION

28 sts and 36 rows to 10 cm square on 3¼mm needles (or size needed to obtain given tension).

BACK

With MC and 2¾mm needles cast on 106 (112: 120: 126) sts.
Work in K2 P2 rib. for 2 in. (5 cm).
Change to 3¼mm needles and starting with a K row, work in st. st. At the same time inc. 1 st. at both ends on next and every foll. 10th row until 132 (138: 146: 152) sts. Work 1 row.

○ To shape armholes

*Dec 1 st. (3 stitches from edge) at both ends on next and foll. 6 alt. rows. [118 (124: 132: 138) sts.] * Work straight until armhole measures 10 in (25 cms) ending with a P row.

○ To shape shoulders

Cast off 7 (7: 8: 8) sts. at beg. of next 8 rows, and 6 (8: 7: 9) sts. at beg. next 2 rows.
Leave rem. 50 (52: 54: 56) sts on a holder.

FRONT

Work as given for back until work measures 5½ in (14 cm). from beg. ending with a P row. [114 (120: 128: 134) sts].

Next row – K8 (11: 15: 18) sts, K 1st row of patt. from chart, K to end of row.
Next row – P8 (11: 15: 18) sts, P 2nd row of patt. from chart, P to end of row.
Cont. working rows of patt. from chart as placed, and inc. 1 st. at both ends of every 10th row as before to 132 (138: 146: 152) sts. Work 1 row.

○ To shape armholes

Work as given for back from * to *, keeping patt. as set.
Work straight until armhole measures 8 in (20 cm).

○ To shape neck

With RS facing, K47 (49: 52: 54) sts, turn, leave rem. sts. on a spare needle.
**Dec. 1 st. at neck edge on the next 13 rows. Work straight until length measures same as back to shoulder, ending at armhole edge.

○ To shape shoulder

Cast off 7 (7: 8: 8) sts at beg. of next and foll. 3 alt. rows.
Work 1 row. Cast off 6 (8: 7: 9) sts.
With RS work facing, slip next 24 (26: 28: 30) sts onto a holder. Rejoin yarn to next st. and K to end of row.
Complete to match first side from ** to end.

SLEEVES

With 2¾mm needles cast on 64 sts and work 2½ in (6 cm) in K2 P2 rib.
Change to 3¼mm needles and starting with a K row, work in st. st. At the same time inc. 1 st. at both ends on next and foll. 11 alt. rows [88 sts].
Then every foll. 4th row until there are 140 sts.
Work straight until sleeve measures 17½ (17½: 18: 18½) in, 44 (44: 46: 47) cm from beg. ending with a P row.

○ To shape top

Dec. 1 st. at both ends on next and foll. 6 alt. rows. [126 sts]. Work 1 row. Cast off.

NECKBAND

Sew up left shoulder.
With 2¾mm needles, pick up and K50 (52: 54: 56) sts. from back neck, 26 sts

from left side neck, 24 (26: 28: 30) sts from centre front and 26 sts from right side neck [126 (130: 134: 138) sts].
Work 2 in (5 cm) in K2 P2 rib. Cast off loosely in rib.

TO MAKE UP

Press work according to yarn instructions, omitting ribbing.
Sew up right shoulder and neckband.
Fold neckband in half and sew down on wrong side.
Sew in sleeves. Sew up side and sleeve seams.

KISSING TIME

This roll-necked mini-dress is waiting for a kiss!

MATERIALS

Yarn 7 (7: 8: 8) × 50g 4 ply main colour (blue)
Small amounts Contrasts A – red, B – pink, C – green, D – yellow.
Needles 1 pair 2¾mm (UK 12)
1 pair 3¼mm (UK 10)

MEASUREMENTS

To fit bust 30 (32: 34: 36) in, 76 (81: 87: 92) cm.
Length 37½ (37½: 39½: 39½) in, 95 (95: 100: 100) cm.
Sleeve seam 17½ (17½: 18: 18½) in, 44 (44: 46: 47) cm.

TENSION

28 sts and 36 rows to 10 cm square on 3¼mm needles (or size needed to obtain given tension).

BACK

With 2¾mm needles and MC cast on 98 (106: 112: 120) sts.
Work 12 (12: 14: 14) in, 30 (30: 35: 35) cm in K1, P1 rib.
Change to 3¼mm needles and starting with a K row, work in st. st. At the same time inc. 1 st. at both ends on next and every foll. 10th row until 124 (132: 138: 146) sts. Work 1 row.

○ To shape armholes

★ Dec 1 st. (3 stitches from edge) at both ends on next and foll. 6 alt. rows [110 (118: 124: 132) sts]. ★ Work straight until armhole measures 10 in (25 cm) ending with a P row.

○ To shape shoulders

Cast off 6 (7: 7: 8) sts at beg. of next 8 rows, and 6 (6: 7: 7) sts at beg. of next 2 rows.
Leave rem. 50 (50: 54: 54) sts. on a holder.

FRONT

Work as given for back until work measures 19¼ (19¼: 21¼: 21¼) in, 49 (49: 54: 54) cm. from beg. ending with a P row.

[112 (120: 126: 134) sts].
Next row – K22 (26: 29: 33) sts, K. 1st row of patt. from chart, K to end of row.
Next row – P23 (27: 30: 34) sts, P 2nd row of patt. from chart, P to end of row.
Cont. working rows of patt. from chart as placed, and inc. 1st at both ends of every 10th row as before to 124 (132: 138: 146) sts. Work 1 row.

○ To shape armholes

Work as given for back from ★ to ★, keeping patt. as set. Work straight until armhole measures 8 in. (20 cm).

○ To shape neck

With RS facing K44 (47: 49: 53) sts, turn, leave rem. sts. on a spare needle.
★★ Dec. 1 st. at neck edge on the next 13 (13: 14: 14) rows.
Work straight until length measures same as back to shoulder ending at armhole edge.

○ To shape shoulder

Cast off 6 (7: 7: 8) sts at beg. of next and foll. 3 alt. rows. Work 1 row. Cast off 6 (6: 7: 7) sts.
With RS work facing, slip next 24 (24: 26: 26) sts. onto a holder. Rejoin yarn to next st. and K to end of row.
Complete to match first side from ★★ to end.

SLEEVES

With 2¾mm needles and MC cast on 64 sts. Work 2 in (5 cm) in K1 P1 rib.
Change to 3¼mm needles and starting with a K row, work in st. st. At the same time inc. 1 st. at both ends on next and foll. 11 alt. rows, [88 sts], then every foll. 4th row until 140 sts.
Work straight until sleeve measures 17½ (17½: 18: 18½) in, 44 (44: 46: 47) cm. from beg. ending with a p. row.

○ To shape top

Dec. 1 st. at both ends on next and foll. 6 alt. rows. [126 sts]. Work 1 row. Cast off.

ROLL NECKBAND

Sew up left shoulder.
With 3¼mm needles, pick up and K50 (50: 54: 54) sts. from back neck, 26 (26: 28: 28) sts. from left side neck, 24

(24: 26: 26) sts. from centre front and 26 (26: 28: 28) sts. from right side neck. [126 (126: 136: 136) sts].
Starting with a P row, work 30 rows in rev. st. st.
Cast off.

TO MAKE UP

Press work according to yarn instructions, omitting ribbing and roll neckband. Sew up right shoulder and neckband. Hold neckband in place with a few stitches at shoulder seams. Sew in sleeves. Sew up side and sleeve seams.

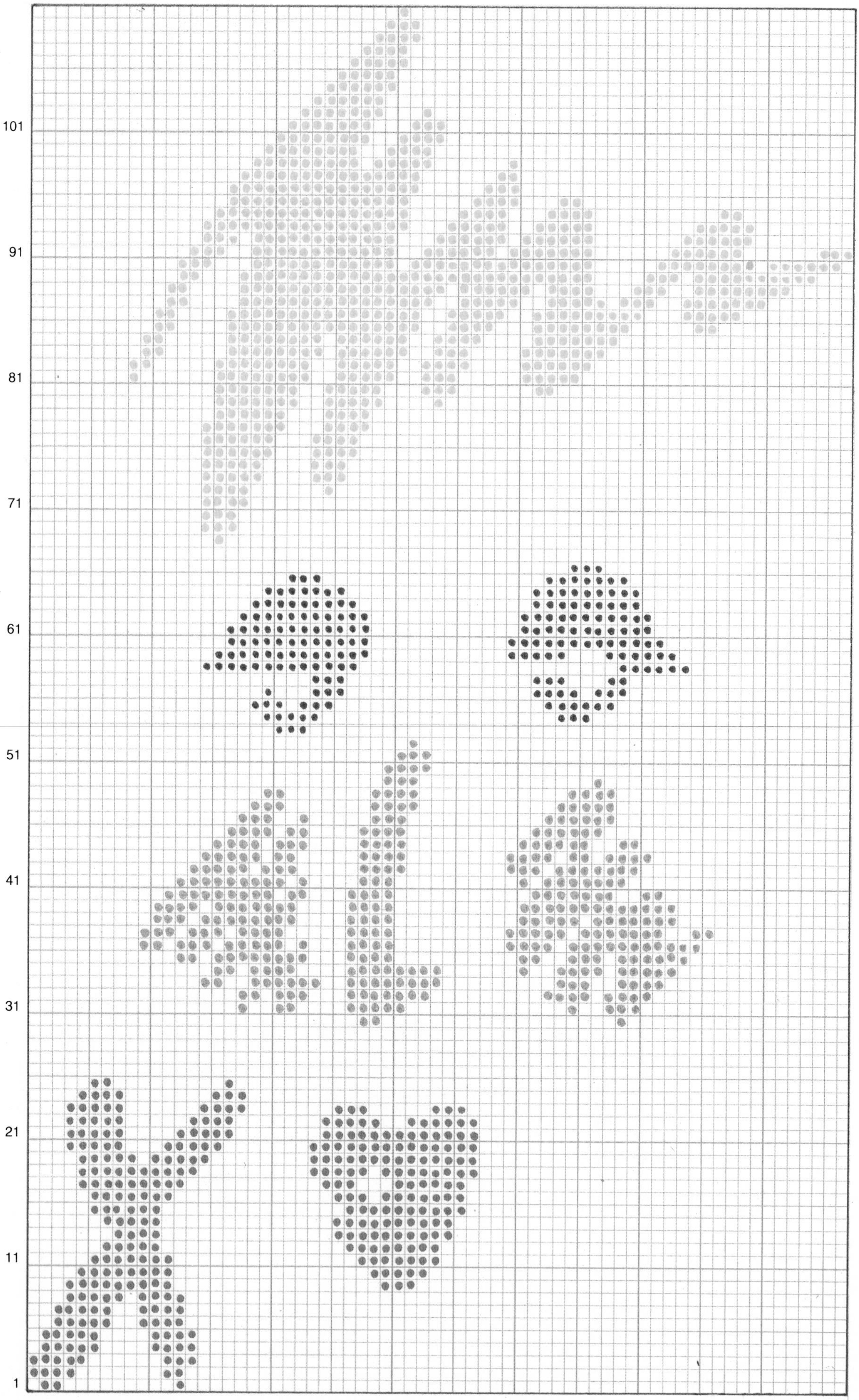
101
91
81
71
61
51
41
31
21
11
1

TRENDSETTER

A plain mini-dress and roll-edged vest in brilliant contrasting colours. The dress can be worn on its own, and the vest can be worn over a shirt or another sweater. To knit the dress follow the instructions for Kissing Time (page 87) omitting the pattern.

ROLL-EDGED VEST

MATERIALS

Yarn 3 (3: 4: 4) × 50g 4 ply main colour
1 × 50g contrast A
Needles 1 pair 3¼mm (UK 10)

MEASUREMENTS

To fit bust 30 (32: 34: 36) in, 76 (81: 87: 92) cm (fits loosely).
Length 17½ in, 45cm.

TENSION

28 sts and 36 rows to 10 cm square on 3¼mm needles (or size needed to obtain given tension).

BACK

With MC cast on 140 (148: 154: 162) sts. Starting with a K row, work 9 rows in st. st., then K1 row to make fold line for hem. Cont. straight and in st. st. for a further 6½ in (17 cm) ending with a P row.

○ **To shape armholes**
Cast off 7 sts at beg. of next 2 rows, then dec. 1 st. at both ends of next and foll 6 alt. rows. [112 (120: 126: 134) sts].
Work straight until armhole measures 10 in (25 cm) ending with a P row.

○ **To shape shoulders**
Cast off 5 (6: 6: 7) sts at beg. of next 8 rows, and 5 (5: 6: 6) sts. at beg. of next 2 rows.
Leave rem. 62 (62: 66: 66) sts. on a holder.

FRONT

Work as given for back until work measures 3½ in (9 cm) from fold line for hem, ending with a P row.
Next row – K26 (30: 33: 37) sts, K 1st row of patt. from chart, K to end of row.
Next row – P32 (36: 39: 43) sts, P 2nd row of patt. from chart, P to end of row.
Cont. working rows of patt. from chart

as placed. At the same time when work measures same as back to armholes shape armholes.

○ **To shape armholes**
Work as for back.
When patt. rows completed, work 1 row the shape neck as follows.

○ **To shape neck**
With RS facing K43 (47: 48: 52) sts, turn, leave rem sts. on a spare needle. ★
Dec 1 st. at neck edge on the next 18 rows. Work straight until length measures same as back to shoulder ending at armhole edge.

○ **To shape shoulder**
Cast off 5 (6: 6: 7) sts at beg. of next and foll. 3 alt. rows.
Work 1 row. Cast off 5 (5: 6: 6) sts.
With RS facing slip next 26 (26: 30: 30) sts onto a holder.
Rejoin yarn to next st. and K to end of row.
Complete to match first side from ★ to end.

NECKBAND

Join left shoulder seam.
With RS work facing pick up and K62 (62: 66: 66) sts from back neck, 28 sts. from left side neck, 26 (26: 30: 30) sts from centre front and 28 sts. from right side neck.
[144 (144: 152: 152) sts]. Starting with a P row, work 34 rows in rev. st. st. Cast off.

○ **Armhole edging**
Join right shoulder and neckband.
With RS facing, pick up and K156 along armhole edge.
Starting with a P row, work 20 rows in rev. st. st. Cast off.
Work other armhole edge to match.

TO MAKE UP

Press work according to yarn instructions omitting neckband and armhole edging. Sew up side seams and armhole edging. Hold neckband and armhole edging in place with a few stitches at shoulders and underarm seams respectively. Slip stitch hem up on wrong side.

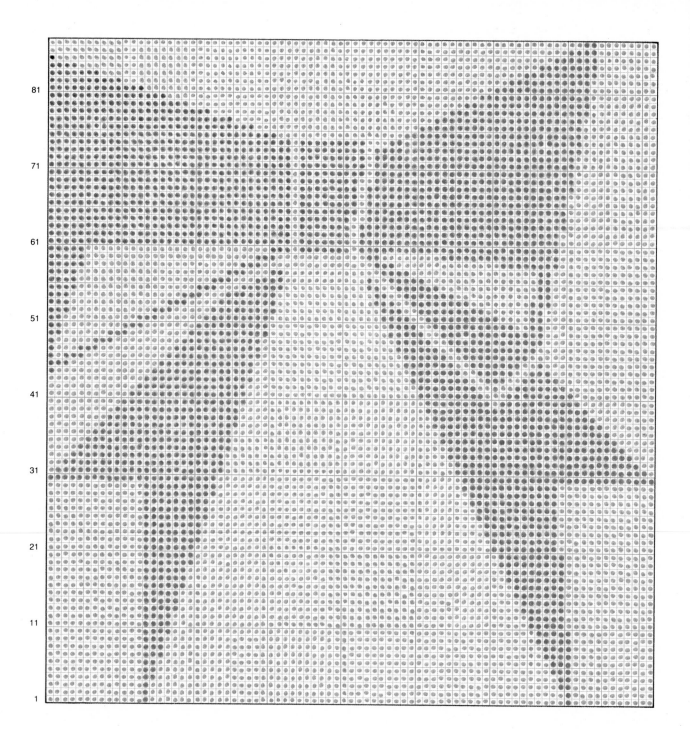

DO IT YOURSELF
ALPHABET

This alphabet can be used if you wish to add words of your own to any of the patterns, or to change those given in the patterns.

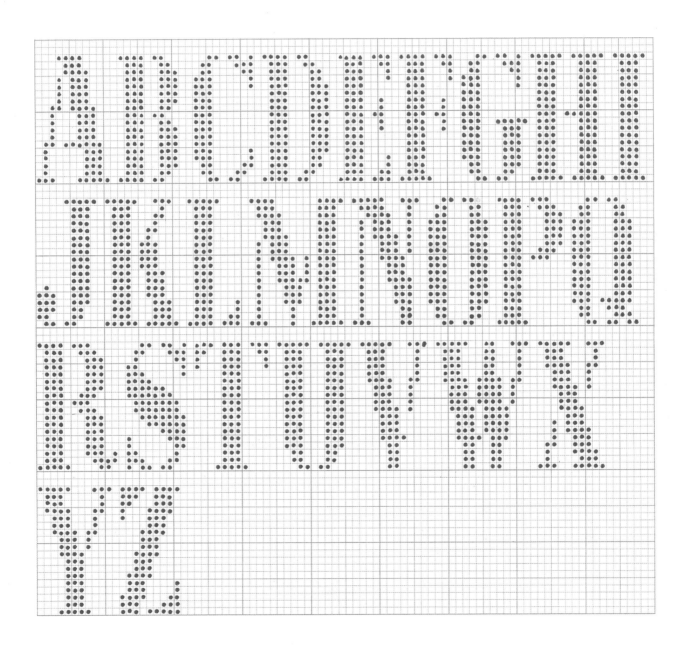